Perception Is Key

Perception Is Key

How Leaders Today Can Navigate Workplace Politics

Richard D. Tomko

ROWMAN & LITTLEFIELD
Lanham • Boulder • New York • London

Published by Rowman & Littlefield
An imprint of The Rowman & Littlefield Publishing Group, Inc.
4501 Forbes Boulevard, Suite 200, Lanham, Maryland 20706
www.rowman.com

6 Tinworth Street, London SE11 5AL, United Kingdom

British Library Cataloguing in Publication Information Available

Library of Congress Cataloging-in-Publication Data Available

ISBN 978-1-4758-5391-9 (cloth)
ISBN 978-1-4758-5392-6 (pbk)
ISBN 978-1-4758-5393-3 (electronic)

I am dedicating this book to my children Maya, Max, Molly, and Marco. Throughout our lives as parents, we do all we can to navigate our careers and our personal interactions hoping to be perceived by others as one of the "greats." The hardest job, with the greatest satisfaction, that I have ever had is being their father, but I always work harder at just being "dad." It will be my ultimate success story to watch them navigate their own lives and each have their own success—whatever that definition may be.

Every Battle Is Won Before It Is Ever Fought

—Sun Tzu

Contents

Foreword

I first met Rich Tomko shortly after taking on my dream job—the ultimate leadership role! No longer would I be a spectator. It took me eight years to get to this point in my "career," and I wasn't going to mess this up. I would do whatever it takes.

I soon found out that Rich was going to be part of our team and my right-hand man—my assistant. He is a big burly guy, walks with confidence, "He surely knows what he is doing." I, on the other hand, was faking it. I had to give off the perception that I knew the game, for heaven sake I was in charge because I was the coach!

Yes, my dream job at the time was coaching my third-grade daughter in soccer. I have a very successful career in business but this job meant so much more. The greatest challenge was I had never played or coached soccer. By looking at Rich, I knew he too was an American football "guy," but with his confidence and command of the soccer parents, I just assumed he coached the sport prior to that season. The reality is that was far from the truth.

He and I entered into the "C suite" (coaching suite) both as novices. Throughout that entire season, we leveraged our professional experiences and backgrounds in business, politics, education, and sometimes—the art of persuasion—to navigate victory and the belief that we knew what we were doing. Perception and polioptics matter in every environment.

I have a twenty-five-year career as a global executive in both the logistics and technology sectors. I started my career driving a truck—literally. I navigated my way through nineteen promotions over the course of those years, moving from a successful truck driver to the head of a global digital solutions organization.

In this book, Rich writes the truth. Though we all would like to think that working hard and showing exceptional performance in our job is all that should matter, the "truth" is once you reach a certain level of technical competence how you navigate office workplace politics makes all the difference.

Rich does what all politically savvy people do. He asks the hard, inquisitive questions, and shares many of the answers to those questions in this book. Over his many years as an educator, business leader, politician, and "coach," he has learned and mastered the art of perception, and he has a great understanding and expertise in the topics he writes about. After reading *Perception Is Key: How Leaders Today Can Navigate Workplace Politics*, you will soon come to realize that workplace politics is definitely not a spectator sport.

Raymond E. Aschenbach
Senior Vice President, Global Digital Solutions
Iron Mountain

Preface

Cleaning for the Cleaning Lady[1]

Every one of us has done it. Well, at least those of us who have either grown up with having (or now in our adult lives hired) a "cleaning lady" to help do the heavy cleaning around the house. "Cleaning people are coming tomorrow," my wife would announce on that same day every month letting the kids and I know that we were all pitching in to straighten up the house before they arrived the next morning. Although the ritual seems like a strange phenomenon it actually makes complete sense. No one wants the cleaning lady to think that he or she is that "messy."

Thus, we live day in and day out in the same conditions until the night before we have hired someone to make those conditions better. And as the cleaning team enters your domain, they let out a sigh of relief—"Ahhhh, what a neat family." You were successful—you have created the perfect perception for the right audience. Although the subtitle of the preface outlines an interesting paradox, the deeper meaning transcends that the appropriate utilization of perception is an important predictor of a person's positive interactions with others.

Specifically, in any leadership or managerial role, an individual's or stakeholder group's perception of how one handles his or her role as a leader can be seen as an extremely valuable tool. This holds true for all types of leadership positions from private sector business and government officials to education and other public administrative roles—perception is powerful.

Throughout our everyday lives, we continuously perceive people in both positive and negative ways. When we first meet an individual, a first impression usually outlines the path of the relationship from that day forward or until some other action causes us to change our feelings about that person.

The individual's actions, reactions, gestures, and overall body language cause one to "paint a picture" of how that individual handles both himself and specific situations surrounding his actions toward others. It is most times what we think to be true about others that causes us to predict what is occurring in his or her everyday life.

I often equate this way of thinking to how a person in a leadership role hires an applicant for a particular job. Of course, she does her vetting of the candidates, verifies points of the resume, and screens those individuals who on paper really "look" great. There was a point circa the late 1990s that colleges were helping students with resume writing and insisting that fancier paper made one "stand out" as an applicant.

I'm sure there is someone out there who would still argue that point. I guess one could agree that different actions create different results and the first step in any career future is to be noticed. Thus, while noticing this attractive resume, she figured its contents meet the tenets of her search, and she calls the candidate in for a formal interview.

Although interview structures throughout different industries vary, the goal is the same. Management wants to find the best possible candidate for the position that is available in their company, school, office, etc. But what will they really be viewing during this interview? Sure, the resume reads of the right things, and the candidate's references—well, unless the screener is calling someone "off the sheet," she is calling a reference that knows to be expecting a call. So how does one truly know how productive this candidate will be without him even spending five minutes on the job?

Simple. You don't.

What is studied and decided upon on are "triggers" that allow the interview panel to place the person in that position and ultimately be successful. Triggers such as appearance; organization; the ability to seemingly work well with others; resume pedigree; experience; and overall likeability. Most, if not all, of these triggers deal with perception and how the individual is perceived as he is being vetted. This sense of knowing how one is perceived and how to navigate the areas where perception is most important is what will indicate and measure success in any field or industry career within the global marketplace.

The greatest perception anomaly in leadership is the idea that a leader or manager, who enters a new workplace solely and for the first time as a leader, had to be the most incredible and productive middle manager, worker, and so on in that field in order to get the position. In other words, it is easily implied and perceived that someone assumes a role because she has had the success, training, and track record to have been recruited for such a prominent and important position. This phenomenon can more easily be termed "starting over."

Regardless of what occurs deep within the lines of one's resume, it all seems to "disappear" once she walks out of her old office en route to her next destination. Sure, social media and news items will help to define the past, but in a general sense she will start her new title with a clean slate being perceived that she is the ultimate candidate to lead or work in that new position.

Conversely, an individual who is promoted to a position from within an organization is facing a double-edged sword. On the one side, he can be perceived as worthy of switching offices and leading his team, where on the other, he may be seen as unqualified, conspiring, and downright undeserving of the position. Although there are several learning curves that colleagues can truly understand, there are actions and interactions that will be analyzed and dissected for better or worse.

So, here is why perception is the key to navigating workplace politics. Simply stated, if an individual can learn to identify the areas where being perceived in a positive manner has the most effect on growing respect and loyalty for herself by others and then she understands how to maneuver around and manipulate an individual's perception of her in consideration of those areas, she will be overly successful in handling the true matters and dilemmas she may face in considering the politics and culture of her workplace.

At the same time, she will help mold her work environment and culture to provide a path to longevity for both the organization and herself as she contributes to growing the mission to include her own ideals and values. Isn't that the goal? To ensure that as we exit one "life," one moment, one career, and as we move from one place to the next we leave our legacy behind for future generations to gain benefit and then morph into their own legacies? How one is perceived is important in being able to see this through and that level of importance will only increase with experience and time.

We still clean for the cleaning lady now decades later. She knows it, and why should she complain? She loves being part of our "team," because she knows we take pride in performance and work hard at formulating how we are perceived by others. That's why she feels successful—because she knows we care about her and her ability to perform her service.

Well, at least she perceives it to be that way.

NOTE

1. The term "Lady" is meant as a reference to a whimsical term for a fictitious character. In no way does this reference any gender biases or disrespect for the professional as a whole.

Acknowledgment

The pages of this book acknowledge the hard work of all of those industry leaders who have put in the time, effort, and dedication to elevate to their positions, understanding that workplace politics and how one is perceived by others played the ultimate role in determining that success. When sitting at the apex of their career, it is very easy to forget all of the disappointments, trials, and tribulations that they faced on the way "up" the proverbial ladder.

It is important to make it a point to remember those trying times, when politics may have prevented them from moving forward and where perception played a role in the decisions that were made for the choices they faced. They must never forget what got them where they are today, and all of the personal, family, and monetary sacrifices that were afforded to reach this point in their professional lives.

Introduction

Why Read This Book?

Leaders and aspiring leaders looking to be successful in their company or organization must accept the role that politics plays in the daily happenings of the workplace. Great leadership includes the ability to not only be competent, educated, and well-versed in the tenets of the role but also be perceived by others as competent in most all aspects of the mission with which he has been charged. At times, using perception appropriately will provide a sense of security that is needed for the leader to navigate political situations accurately and efficiently.

This only truly occurs if he uses perceptive tools and techniques to ensure that he is viewed in a positive light even though he may not be the most qualified in a specific area of his role. It is impossible for one individual to be great at all things; however, an individual can be perceived that way.

The chapters contain theories, best practices, and tried-and-true methods for individuals to recognize and make use of while attempting to find their way through the politics of their workplace and to compete with others who use politics as a catalyst to motivate, restrict, or coerce coworkers and higher level leaders into perceiving themselves in a certain way.

Perception is key for any individual who is wanting to utilize his strengths and core values to help promote a change within an organization; formulate a strong and positive stance for how he is viewed by others at his job or within his company; motivate others into thinking he may be more prepared or competent in an area where he may not be as strong; enhance how others view him in consideration of future leadership or management roles; and grow strong alliances due to how he is respected and revered by colleagues, coworkers, and subordinates.

Chapter 1

Politics 101

Politics can be defined as the way individuals living and working within specific groups make decisions. As a pure definition, the term "politics" usually refers to the way that countries are governed and how a government works to make rules, statutes, and laws. Politics is also seen and relevant in the everyday operations and mission of other groups, such as corporations, non-profit organizations, companies, clubs, educational institutions, and places of worship.

Politics also plays a role in our personal lives, both while at home and most definitely while in the workplace. It may not be as upfront as one would expect, but the underlying principles are present on a daily basis. There is always an expectation by many that things are only political if they are backed by a politician or through some government entity.

In fact, nearly every decision that is made in our lives which includes some type of influencer has politics attached to it. Whether one has leverage or not, using the ability to position one need over another, or to acquire something of value over something that can be exchanged, causes individuals to intuitively use political "muscle" to enhance their lives. When we discuss personal politics and relationships, a different dynamic sets in since there are many more feelings and long-lasting connections that can muddy the waters.

However, although similarities definitely exist, politics in the workplace are navigated through posturing and productivity which is only visible through the lens of perception.

POLITICAL LANDSCAPE

Learning and navigating the political landscape in any workplace relationship should be a top priority for the student of politics. This includes not only an ability to predict partnerships but also to identify which alliances are already established and any tendrils to connections of the primary relationship.

Initially, laying out the landscape allows one to understand how these connections work in tandem when decisions are made or influence is needed. Just as important, being able to identify connections will assist the student of politics when knowing what to—or what not to—say, or to establish a pattern of how he should act around certain individuals. Even though the "when" is also extremely important, knowing the "who" and "how" is much more beneficial when navigating the political atmosphere of the workplace.

Further, it is imperative that he becomes aware of how, when, and why the landscape changes as alliances do tend to ebb and flow on a very consistent basis. In stating this, it is also worth noting that he should pay specific attention to the reasons behind the changes in political affiliations so as to be able to use, or at least recall, those reasons to his advantage in the near and distant future.

Politics must be codependent with patience, as most decisions and bonds take time to secure and ensure they are strong enough to survive the landscape at that time. This dependency also includes the ability to thoroughly vet individuals, their alliances, strengths, and weaknesses in order to offer the best possible course of action while navigating the landscape.

POLITICAL WILL

One must be agile and versatile when politics rears its head in the workplace. The ability to adapt and be prepared to respond to any situation that comes about in consideration of the overarching tenets of the organization can lead to a successful run at securing what one needs most to be successful at work. It is overly important that the individual remains savvy when plotting the political culture of the "office," and not be seen as purely political. Yes, there is a major difference.

In any type of politics, being politically savvy is evidenced through an individual's competent knowledge, the mapping of the landscape through an understanding and pinpointing of specific nuances, and the relationships between individuals and the decisions they make to help motivate others. Having that savviness evidenced proves the individual has been promoted from "student" to "player" within the political arena.

Being savvy is understanding the outcomes that stem from observed interactions. Being political is when one's actions are used to dictate the outcomes. Using actions to force change is an extremely dangerous use of politics. At first, the action will greatly benefit the individual and increase her political capital. However, time will ultimately change the direction of politics through struggle, differences in opinion, power play, and strife. Then, those individual faces in positions of interest who initially supported the political action will either change or be influenced by others.

WORKPLACE POLITICS DEFINED

One would think that certain industries and careers wouldn't be encapsulated by politics. One would be wrong. In fact, the most unsuspecting fields usually envelop the most political atmospheres. This especially holds true where labor unions and bargaining units have oversight over the operations and conditions of the daily working environment. This is not to suggest that these organizations hinder progress due to their involvement.

On the contrary, providing a system of checks-and-balances between workers and management has been proven to advance productivity and enhance the growth of workplace culture and relatability. Rather, it is important to recognize the political factors involved and the compromise needed to ensure a smooth transition from one need to the next.

Take the field of education, for example. How can a field, determined to provide instruction and training to better the lives of individuals of all ages and ensure the future is more productive than the past, include any political mechanisms that would only serve to thwart progress? Here, the answer seems peculiar, but simple. The recipe for any successful education system includes all of the major, necessary political ingredients to thicken the primordial "soup" that nourishes society.

Simply stated, by mixing children, funding, assessment benchmarks, taxes, management, and labor, politics and posturing ensue. Similar situations occur in public works, non-profit charities, softball club teams, and small parent–teacher associations across the country. Circling back, understanding the politics of any workplace will give an individual the edge needed when vying for a successful career in any industry. In the forthcoming chapters, the pages will describe for the reader how important it is for an individual to control how she is perceived by others in order to navigate workplace politics in an effective manner.

CHECKING FOR UNDERSTANDING

How Are You Perceived?

- How important of a role has politics played in your past and current personal and professional lifestyle?
- What types of political maneuvers can hurt aspiring leaders in the workplace? How?
- When is the utilization of politics safe?

Chapter 2

Perception in Workplace Politics

A person can argue that individuals subconsciously realize how perception plays an integral role in their own lives. Even young children understand that it is socially important how a friend perceives them in order to maintain those friendships, grow new friendships, and gain a certain desired status within any social circle. In knowing this, we also recognize that there is a transition somewhere into adulthood where we decide that perception becomes even more of an influence not only in our personal lives but in our professional lives as well.

For many of us (if not most), it becomes extremely necessary to be perceived by others as successful, well-liked, a person with an inviolable moral compass, and just an overall strong individual in every sense of the term. In the same way that someone's definitive style has the ability to mold his or her interactions with others, perception in and of itself can help someone gain or lose prospective clients, money, relationships, friendships, and even her own self-worth.

Spending close to thirty years in leadership roles in non-profit, governmental, and private business organizations, I can tell you that one thing is certain—perception plays a major role when an individual is attempting to navigate workplace politics. For most people, perception becomes reality. This may not be an optimal statement, but it is the truth. Therefore, when dealing with others it is very important to understand how perception plays a strong part in molding relationships and giving someone the ability to ensure that a goal is attainable and will be reached as long as you are involved.

It must also be stated that perception is not solely defined by physical "looks." Although someone's image is an extremely important ingredient when creating a successful recipe, perception includes not only image and style but the way an individual carries himself, speaks with others, organizes

7

a schedule, and the way he manages relationships. In fact, it is necessary for an individual to recognize what his weaknesses are in an attempt to strengthen the way he may be perceived by others.

What better to work on than those strong personality traits, or flaws, that others perceive to be detrimental to a successful "you"? Thus, it takes a leader with some very thick skin to utilize constructive measures and strong criticism to grow from and effectuate change in consideration of gaining power and influence over others.

Perception is real. Understandably, that does sound not only confusing but odd. However, it is the plight of most human beings to be either optimistic and believe that all people are wholesome or good, or pessimistic and believe that all people are bad, until an individual proves to be otherwise. Prior to any fact-checking, research, or analysis, how one individual perceives another is how that relationship—and the individual—will be viewed. Therefore, it is extremely important to understand that first impressions, for different events and engagements, are what will cause how a leader is perceived by others, overall.

Not fair? Well, too bad. Another successful lesson in navigating workplace politics is knowing when to accept that things just won't be fair—or go "your way"—and using that reality to your advantage. It is understandable why leaders have a difficult time recognizing how they are perceived. First, an immediate flaw of many individuals who elevate to leadership roles is that they tend to let their guard down, knowing now that they have gained some sense of power over other individuals.

Rather, a sidecar for any new leadership positions should include a humbling sense of the leader looking outside-inside, attempting to understand or discover how other individuals perceive him as a leader. This becomes difficult for individuals who elevate from other internal positions within a company for several reasons. An individual, who may have been promoted from inside an organization, company, or corporate department, has created a certain persona for himself as a daily worker.

The conversations, theories, stories, etc. that were made don't go "away" when one puts on the team leader hat. For example, if the individual was someone who established a strong rapport with his co-workers and they all collectively "dressed down" on Fridays, it is difficult to expect that now, since he is in command, that his friends will all put a tie on to end the work week.

Second, individuals who know the new leader from the "inside" know what his weaknesses are and how he has handled issues stemming from those weaknesses in the past. When he elevates, he will automatically be seen (and rightly so) as still having those weaknesses. This doesn't mean that this will lead to an automatic failure as he begins his leadership trail. Rather, it is important that he recognizes that this is how he will be perceived so that he can utilize other methods and attenuate his leadership style to create a successful transition.

For those individuals who enter a new organization or company structure for the first time in a management or leadership role, they will immediately be challenged to prove themselves in the role; however, they will also be perceived by those loyal members of the company or firm as being successful leaders since the current employees couldn't imagine the chief officer hiring someone who wasn't the most qualified or successful applicant in the candidate pool.

Here, that type of perception becomes reality when that leader proves she has the ability to lead the team, leading through example and modeling the actions she wants her team to produce. In other words, if the new mission is to sell an extra 1,000 widget units per week, the new leader will make how she is perceived a reality by showing herself in the trenches with the sales team, mobilizing through production, and working with her business department on the financial impact of sales.

By putting the theory into practice, the perception of her experience, expertise, and success outside of the new workplace becomes a heightened reality and advances her political and leadership capital tremendously among her subordinates. However, a new leader must also be aware of and ensure that this near immediate approval rating doesn't upset the political landscape "above" her and she doesn't mismanage the workplace politics important for her own survival, trajectory of success in the organization, and her future ability to enjoy some upward mobility in the leadership hierarchy.

Understanding workplace politics and how one is perceived by others while attempting to navigate through such matters is winning half the battle of becoming a successful leader in any business or industry. Perception and its influence on nearly every situation that surrounds one's lifestyle and working relationships are behaviors that can be sharpened, strengthened, and perfected to assist an aspiring or current leader to address and control nearly every situation that he will be entrusted with during his tenure in his role.

Whether it is attempting to prove to a management team that he is ready to join the ranks of the hierarchy in a company; asking townspeople in a small community to elect him to government office; or elevating to a greater leadership role in a private business sector venture, a true master of perception can use communication, techniques, and methods relating to respect and positive rapport to help engage others and influence outcomes.

CHECKING FOR UNDERSTANDING

How Are You Perceived?

- Do you feel that you are successful in your current job, occupation, or career industry? Reflect on the current goals you have set for yourself. Where do you see yourself in five years?
- Whether your goals lead you to the same company, business, industry, or job that you are currently in or not, how do you think others need to perceive you in order to meet and surpass those goals you have set for yourself in consideration of these: Work ethic? Relationships? Knowledge of job-sense?

Chapter 3

Why Do We Cut Our Grass?

It is important to understand why we must analyze the reasoning behind our utilization of perceptive measures and how perception relates to many of the tenets of leadership and the management of organizational systems throughout business and industry. Every day, the perception that others have about us helps to promote an awareness of how we intrinsically feel about the success, or lack thereof, we are determining for ourselves in that given moment in time.

Individuals will claim that what other people think about them isn't what's important—it's what/how one feels about oneself that truly matters in today's society. Although it can be argued that an individual's choices when considering a multitude of different areas can dictate how he feels about himself, it must also be presented that an individual's style and "taste" makes him unique in compared to others. These are the things in his life that make him stand out from the crowd and allow that individual to express himself in order to release a sense of conformity that he has engaged in a typical workday.

However, societal norms or at least those norms that represent a majority view of some typical sense of acceptance and "normalcy" are an important representation that we are aware that there is a litmus test of sorts that individuals utilize to gauge some level of competency for an individual within a consideration of multiple measures. We all, in turn, understand that meeting these norms may in no way dictate our true inner-self, but will ensure a level of acceptance with groups such as our neighbors, co-workers, or even extended family members for that matter.

This is why a person cuts his grass. The level of intensity, professional assistance requested, and expenses incurred when landscaping a property provides enough variables for an individual to feel a sense of autonomy in creating his own design, vision, and awareness so that he maintains his property while making a statement about himself, whatever that statement may be.

Regardless of what is happening beyond that front yard, inside the house, or in consideration of what that house looks like inside, the desire and need for a reaction from others due to this attempt at "curb appeal" is not only for personal gratification but can be used as a marker for viable social accolades as visitors perceive your grass to mean that you have a lot of money (or you don't); the inside of your house must be extravagant (or isn't); you must be very neat and tidy (or very messy); and you must truly care about what others think of you.

Perception is the key that opens the door to many different reactions from specific stakeholder groups, friends, and family members. The true "art" comes into play when an individual leader knows which key to use and when to "open" the door. It is important for a true leader, or even more an individual searching for a leadership role, to utilize specific reactions from others in order to elicit a perceived reaction or to get an individual (or group of individuals) to perform a specific task while growing her own powerbase.

THE IMPORTANCE OF PERCEPTION IN LEADERSHIP

As a young leader in the field of educational administration, I worked my way through the proverbial "chairs" and learned from some of the best leaders in education at the time, and even more from some of the most unsuccessful individuals I have ever been associated with. I learned early on that although a strong knowledge base definitely helped these individuals through all of the pedagogical dialogue, programs, and each had in our "field," it truly was how these individuals were perceived by others as to how successful or unsuccessful they were in consideration of not only their overall leadership value, but even when completing a single, specific task that needed stakeholder buy-in.

In the early part of 2002, I was a young administrator working in a small, suburban, blue-collared community where the chief officer of our organization was working with the community to renovate building space and advance the mission of the local school district. He entered my office one day and after a friendly exchange, he got right to the point. "Rich," he said. "I need you to take a vacation day Friday."

A bit perplexed, I inquired a little more, and he continued to explain that he really needed my help laying cement in one of the new laboratories because we needed to save some money on the project. He went on to report that every other building leader was going to help out, and it would really be great if I would lend a hand that day, on my own time, as well. Not only was I the newest administrator in the township which meant I really didn't have an actual choice in the matter, I was actually excited to be part of this project.

I distinctly remember thinking how this was the most caring boss I ever worked for, wanting me to work with the team for the greater good of the community. Word quickly "got out" on how the administrative staff and the chief officer were going to help pour foundation for new laboratories over the weekend, and the news truly spread like wildfire. No one seemed to question it or even the liability of staff assisting with a project of this nature with absolutely no expertise in the area of construction. We were pencil pushers— the "suits." But that wasn't out of some sense of fear, uneasiness, or just our being lazy. To the contrary, we did it because he wanted us to.

So the task as explained was simple, but the labor wasn't. We were to "rake" cement as it flowed freely into the classroom through an outside window while seasoned masons formed what was the laboratory subfloor. I came to work on vacation that Friday and saw the construction apparatus set up in the south wing of the campus. Making my way through the hall, I approached the science wing and saw our chief, holding his metal rake in hand and dressed in a pair of old, tattered jeans.

Although I knew he was still my boss, for that minute he made me perceive him as an equal. He made me understand that the project itself was more important than the titles we held and the experience we had. In that instance, he made me understand that he respected me as well and that no one, who was asked to lay cement that day, was better than any other person in that room. The perception was real—the lesson was intense.

Cement began to flow through the discharging chute that was positioned through the laboratory window, and I stood raking the cement alongside our chief. I remember watching him frantically moving the cement back-and-forth and saying to myself, "wow, he's working pretty hard for an old guy." As the pride of my youth got the best of me and my perception of him working harder or as hard as me made me work just that much faster, taking some of his area as well. He was the boss remember, and I had to prove that I wanted to be part of his team and I knew that what he was selling, I was definitely buying.

After around fifteen minutes, we continued to work the job and the chief went off to take a call. He was the boss, and I remember thinking to myself that someone with such an important job must get contacted all hours of the day. A second load of cement was pulling up, and the masons were leading the way as our team of admins worked to make sure the job was completed. I guess you figured already that the chief never came back. One may think that that would have upset us, but it didn't.

He was a true leader, in almost every sense of that definition. But the perception we all had of him that morning, being one of us in the tattered jeans, just sweating alongside us for only a few minutes really portrayed an important message. It really grew our respect for him as not only our leader but a colleague as well. Someone who still knew what it was like to be "in the trenches." Such power is perception that in the right moment, you can almost achieve any goal, in any enterprise, within any organization.

MEASURING TRUE PERCEPTION

How does one measure if the way he uses perception is effective? First, let's be very clear. Perception is not synonymous with deception. Rather, perception is a specific characteristic that one usually perfects with time and expertise. In fact, advancing one's brand through positive perception is an extremely viable way to navigate through workplace politics. By strict definition, perception is one's own ability to hear, see, or become aware of something through the senses.

Over time, success in using this method can be realized as a leader provides not only the appropriate information relative to a specific topic but ensures a specific manner, or vehicle, to how it is delivered to others. There are several key measures to incorporate in advancing one's stature in any organization specific to perception and workplace politics:

1. Lead by Example—Don't stand in the background. As a leader or someone who is looking to elevate through a leadership position in her workplace, an individual must provide subordinates and co-workers with undeniable evidence that she can also perform the task at hand successfully. Although delegating tasks and duties is an important leadership skill, assigning everything to others and not partaking in any part of the majority of actions being used to describe the successful output of the mission, soon looks as though that individual cannot handle it. Remember that when one enters a new position of leadership, although she may have the "usual" animus felt toward her by other members of the unit organization, the overall perception is that she was chosen because she is obviously the most qualified individual for the position and had success in defining that role. This is more direct when one elevates from within an organization, as individuals have their past record of success, failure, and how that individual handled those specific outcomes, including rewards programs and the ability to make substantial changes in order to ensure appropriate sustainability.
2. Do Appropriate Research. It is important that a leader is perceived as having an appropriate amount of knowledge and background information on any and every topic that he will be addressing within the organization.

With regard to the amount of research necessary to be deemed an expert on any organizational issue, the leader must not only have the history and future goals of the issues at hand, but he must also be ready to engage in any conversation with members of different stakeholder groups.

3. Have a "Stump Speech" Ready at All Times. Truly successful leaders are always ready to discuss the positive performance areas of their organizations, as well as be able to navigate through difficult questions with the correct roadmap. Being able to deliver a message to any constituent group that is solid and extremely fluid gives the perception that the leader has the pulse of the organization, understand the mission and vision that has been established, and has developed several long-term goals to move the organization forward.

4. Look the Part. In order to be successful, one must "look" successful. This doesn't necessarily mean that an individual leader's wardrobe should consist of $500 shirts; rather, it must be perceived that the individual is organized and understands how to incorporate the stature of the position along with their everyday routine. Success in any role can grow when individuals perceive that the leader has their best interest in mind and an absolute "game plan" that is dedicated to moving the organization—as well as each individual—forward. Further, a leader must use an appropriate diction and style of addressing others when addressing crowds and creating written correspondence.

5. Qui tacet consentire videtur—"He who is silent is understood to consent." If any leader yearns to be accepted in her role and respected for her knowledge, it must be perceived that she has a strong "voice" in nearly every aspect of the particular workplace, organization, or field. Silence or an inability to comment is a major weakness when identifying any perceived characteristic of leadership. This holds especially true if the leader finds an opportunity to support her subordinates or co-workers by speaking out against an opposing view. It is just as important for a leader to know when to take advantage of the situation through a response as it is to actually make said response to others. At times, one must "strike while the iron is hot," especially when the topic is can be considered either detrimental or beneficial to your office, workers, or program.

WHEN INDIVIDUALS PERCEIVE A LEADER AS CONFIDENT, HE WILL GROW HIS ABILITY TO LEAD THEM

A weak leader is not someone who individuals will line-up and run through fire for. Rather, a leader must prove himself to his constituent and subordinate groups in order to solidify a strict confidence from others in his ability to lead them. Although confidence in competence will be the overwhelming assessment in consideration of the successful plight of an individual in a leadership role, his utilization of the art of perception and perceived methods of leadership will help him arrive to his goals.

The more that leader is perceived to be successful through evidence from true and tried methods, the more he will grow his own ability to lead effectively. Each method, tactic, and style-point will fill his "toolbox" in order to assist him in finding the correct supports in order to build a foundation of trust and eventually grow that trust into a strong leadership role.

CHECKING FOR UNDERSTANDING

How Are You Perceived?

• How do you think co-workers perceive you in the workplace?
• What can you do to strengthen some of those perceptions?

Chapter 4

Perception Defined across Careers and Industries

Perception plays a major part in the leadership roles of individuals in specific organizations and careers. From private business and the not-for-profit sector, to government positions and educational venues, the art of perception can be viewed in different ways and must be used effectively within specific circumstances.

A truly effective leader is one who is able to recognize a need and use perception to her advantage in any organization of business culture. In order to accomplish this, a leader must fully understand the individuals and the climate around him. Further, an individual must be able to fully navigate the components of his job description efficiently and successfully in order to enable his standing in the organization to permeate into other positions.

Here, the leader's level of expertise will be elevated regardless of whether that leader has the most aptitude in the organization or not. By understanding and excelling in all areas of an individual job description while utilizing "people skills" to lead team members effectively, competence and excelling in a leadership or other hierarchical role is inevitable.

BUSINESS SECTOR

Many private business-sector leaders work in what can be perceived as a "dog-eat-dog" environment. The momentum is fast-paced, the politics are cutthroat and sometimes "dirty," and an expected output of work and production can decide what job security looks like. In the business sector, successful members of leadership teams are perceived to be high-spirited "go-getters" who work hard but play harder to ensure that their intensity level for the team, product, organization, and so on, is always put first. In many specific business industries, it is more prevalent to be considered a blue-collar manager rather than a white-collar boss.

In a sector where the majority of work is labor and production, on-site workers and teams tend to respect a leader more who has definitely worked in the "trenches." A manager, director, or an individual with a leadership role who has never worked in a trade or field but is leading a team toward a goal will feel some resistance especially, if it is perceived that he thinks he knows more than his skilled workers.

The reverse holds true in the white-collared positions where power and influence stem from how objectives are achieved from experience and on the job influencers. Basically, positive results evidence success. The amount of money and capital gained or widgets produced seems to hold more clout and is perceived to stand for greater success than most perspectives on human capital and relationships. Regardless, the influence a leader holds throughout a workplace, in any capacity, is perceived by groups of subordinates and colleagues differently, and it is usually based upon the need to know what the leader can do for the individual as well as the business as a whole.

NON-PROFIT SECTOR

Non-profit sector leaders utilize perception to work as a catalyst toward moving a foundation forward based upon the mission of that organization or foundation. Non-profit organizations are established to assist others in support of a particular cause or the needs of a community.

In leading an organization such as this, it is important for a leader to be perceived as knowing all about the organizational cause as well as ensuring that he understands and supports the mission. Although believing in the vision and mission of the organization is key to the success of any leader, a non-profit sector organization most likely surrounds the mission with some type of philanthropic cause or charity.

A leader in this field must know not only the general information surrounding the topic but also specific data and talking points to highlight achievement and spotlight goals. Without being able to provide a fluid dissertation of the cause at hand and the long- and short-term goals of the non-profit, it will be perceived by most that the cause is not worthwhile or the leader is disconnected.

EDUCATIONAL LEADERSHIP

Using the power of politics and perception in educational leadership constitutes several different layers of importance to the instructional leader. One can strongly argue that politics in the workplace is most rampant in an educational setting due to leaders and boards dealing with large municipal budgets, approving jobs and construction referendums, responsible for the real estate values of homes, and being charged with the future of a community.

When dealing with local citizens or members of a higher education community, the different needs of the organization must match those needs of the multiple constituent bases that a leader reports to. As the leader elevates through the different "chairs" of her tenure in a district or on campus, it is inherently assumed that with her mobility comes this established sense of proficiency in that administrative role.

How she is perceived, however, is a completely different concept and probably the more important understanding in how perception can influence the power an individual wields within an educational setting and how she can grow her ability to lead constituent groups within the organization.

This can be evidenced in greater detail as a comparison is made between the respects a newly appointed educational leader gets when he is "promoted" within a district as opposed to the attention he receives if he was appointed from the "outside." To be frank, receiving a promotion as an internal candidate and moving from worker to manager is a double-edged sword.

On one side, the morale of an organization can expand and be more fluid as individuals inside have a strong belief that a person should be promoted who has worked his own way "up the ladder," while also having worked and experienced the same type of conditions that other employees in the organization have. Internal promotions are further evidence that an individual in the organization's hard work has been noticed by the administration, understanding that "every day is an interview," and the management team does take notice. In this instance, an individual must use all of his tools to navigate workplace politics effectively.

GOVERNMENT

Probably the most important arena in which perception plays an integral role is in consideration of government and elected officials. As we understand in these positions, it is virtually impossible to make everyone "happy" where decisions need to be made about the livelihood of others, budgets, policies, and programs. For every one member of a constituent group who agrees with the actions of an elected or appointed government official, there are two members against the decision.

This doesn't so much have a negative reflection on the individual leader; rather, it is just plain reality that not everyone will agree and be happy with decisions that are made. However, it is important for the leader to ensure others perceive that their concerns or positions are important. This can be accomplished in several ways as we consider how one would "map" certain factions of supporters when making decisions that could affect how a leader is supported when future decisions arise.

As government officials serve the public constituency based on different sectors of need, it is important that the official understands how each group relates to the dilemma at hand. To be perceived as knowing why an outcome is important for each particular group will help to gain a level of respect from those members of the constituency. The leader must anticipate the preferred outcomes and the potential gains and losses for the challenge that the group is facing. To know this is to be perceived as a successful public servant, whether earned, appointed, or elected.

It is just as important to know how not to be perceived in a negative light. As in any argument, one can only gain "ground" by knowing her opponent and his strengths and weaknesses. To understand flaws in an argument and the positives or negatives of a competing side is what truly allows an individual to hone in on weaknesses and understand the preferred method to be used to overpower the argument.

However, being perceived as humble can allow you to attain more popularity points with non-supporters where, although you may know that you have won in an argument, you show an understanding for their cause and an attentiveness to their needs. This means of being perceived goes a very long way when the leader looks for any type of return of investment with regard to human capital and support during a reelection campaign, community resource, and volunteers to disseminate a message.

CHECKING FOR UNDERSTANDING

How Are You Perceived?

- How do you believe a leader should be perceived by others in your work or industry?
- What are some specific actions a leader or individual can take in your occupation, job, or career industry that would make him/her "stand out" from other individuals in the workplace?

Chapter 5

Polioptics

One of the most important terms to understand, utilize, and perfect as an aspiring or elevating leader or manager in any workplace is polioptics. Polioptics is the science of using visual aids to ensure that you or your idea is being perceived in the most beneficial manner possible. To be a true "student" of polioptic persuasion is to be able to set the tone and cause leverage in consideration of any decision through the utilization of images and/or physical actions to prove an intentional point, change someone's view, or solidify support for a particular action or position.

To many in the field, polioptics is the be all and end all to assuring that a leader is perceived in a specific and correct manner indicative of the message he is hoping to convey to others. Period. Thus, if you want to be perceived as having what it takes to deliver a message, brand, program—almost anything—successfully to any constituent group, polioptics must play an intimate role in producing that image.

Good leaders use polioptics nearly all day—every day. Specific industries are more equipped and specialized in polioptics where nearly all constituents and stakeholders are exposed to visual aids in order to force decision-making efforts to land in a specific way. We see the most evidence of this in governmental campaigns and election cycles where the political images of candidates seek to heighten the intensity of voters and other members of a community or purpose in order to make those individuals "feel" a particular way about a purpose or individual candidate.

Particular advertisements or press pieces where a candidate is smiling at children; walking with a hardhat on a construction site; looking intensely at citizens who are conversing with the candidate in public; and shaking hands with other party officials. Remember candidates "kissing babies"? Well, maybe that is not so much supported any longer, but the polioptics which surround that former custom sum it all up.

Public officials at ribbon-cutting ceremonies for new businesses; local mayors throwing out first pitches on Little League opening days around the country; and officials always in the background as tragedy strikes and the cameras are out. Call it what you want, but the tool is polioptics. Without it, a current or aspiring leader doesn't have the complete compilation of tools in her arsenal of tricks to ensure that perception is playing a definitive role in shaping her future success nor in strengthening her support base.

A true pundit in polioptics will explain that to be successful, an individual must have a team behind her in order to perfect this science and utilize it to exponentially grow her status in leadership and around the workplace. As a leader needs to concentrate on the mission at hand and the direction of the business, company, or industry in which she leads, other competent individuals must help her market, schedule, create, and perform a plethora of varying physical and visual strategies to assist in strengthening her message and brand. This may be seen in the form of a campaign team (government); a sales and marketing team (private sector business); a community engagement officer (education); and the list goes on.

IMAGE

Whether walking into the building, being produced on television, or live-streamed across the Web, an individual's image lays the foundation for the structure of polioptics being assembled to assist in navigating workplace politics. Clothing, hair, hygiene, how one walks, etc. are all very indicative of how one carries himself in the public eye or around the office. However, in defining image within the sphere of polioptics, it must also be synonymous with anything visible and "attached" to an individual.

No better example than those individuals who utilize specific name brand items during photoshoots and other public appearances. Even the type of pen someone uses can be considered a polioptic method if it has some definitive symbolism or prompting power behind its appearance. Standing at a podium during an event, speech; where individuals sit (or sit next to) on a dais; backdrops for events; etc. also are important polioptic measures to manage and consider from the simplest to the most extravagant of events.

It is further important to note that it is nearly impossible to be able to control every single instance of polioptic utilization. In other words, there are just too many individual visual aids that can be utilized and manipulated to ensure an appropriate decision can be made in consideration of a message or image you are trying to convey. As this is understandable, it is also necessary to ensure that as many optical tools can be set to have a message "seen" and delivered in an appropriate manner.

To be most successful in this venture, an individual should maintain focus on the central theme of the action and rely on those periphery devices as a secondary concern. As an example, if you are hosting an event and the main focus is on a stage area, the leader and team should concentrate on the message being delivered from the polioptic lens in and around the stage area where the main event is taking place.

This should include attention paid to a backdrop, proper amplification of sound, cleanliness, order of speakers/performances, decorations on stage areas, etc. Even though the surrounding and outside areas of the stage and setting are important, those items are subject to the periphery and are secondary in urgency. The bigger the team, the greater the coverage.

POLIOPTICS AND BEING ORGANIZED

One of the most underestimated polioptical importance is that of the true act of being, or being perceived as looking, organized. When a leader and her team come prepared to/for an event in an organized front, that feeling resonates with every member of the team especially, the leader herself. The fluidity of a program and its pace should be second nature to the team, and one member should know what the other member is doing at all times.

Events, speeches, and programs should be perceived as extremely organized since "advance" teams are established to ensure an appropriate and productive level of production is so prominent that any individual mistake or misstep will be overlooked by an unassuming audience. As organization is one of the optimal skill sets to master in any leadership role, being organized rightfully proves that a leader and her team has a hold on the polioptic lens important to moving the desired mission forward or meeting a certain goal.

ALLIANCES

Alliances with particular groups strengthen the marker of polioptics for a leader when particular conditions are met. These conditions are based on the power presented by the group, its standing within the professional or local arena/market, and how the mission of that group aligns with the goal that is trying to be accomplished. Unfortunately, incorrect utilization or cultivating of particular groups can backfire, and backfire badly, on individuals should the group represent an opinion or vision that is opposite that of the desired change required to ensure the leader is successful.

Regardless, in using alliances to move the mission and mindset forward, an individual leader and her team must perform an appropriate and well-defined vetting structure as well as an assurance from his team that the alliance will somehow benefit the cause. How and with whom the leader has aligned as an ally is important when molding the image that one seeks to ensure political capital can exponentially grow over time.

SLOGANS

A wise man once proclaimed to me that "you can take back a spent arrow, but you can never take back the spoken word." Well, that statement intensifies when the written word is added as well. Slogans, "catch" phrases, and other means of communicating a message that is written and/or displayed are extremely powerful when an individual looks to curry favor with respect to an agenda or goal. Most likely, slogans are political in nature or somehow used to establish a pattern of praise or condemnation for a feeling or particular outcome. Slogan statements should be bold and colorful, both in a visual and diction sense of the term.

ADVERTISEMENTS

What other special tool to be placed in one's polioptic toolbox than an advertisement. To advertise an event, upcoming vote, or spotlight, an individual person or action can be very effective in swaying others to show support for your initiative, program, or a programmatic need while being able to define its importance to your constituents or another group that you are trying to reach. Again, the optics of ads help get the meaning of an event to the correct individuals, and it allows those individuals to solidify their support or denial of the matter presented to them.

SCENERY

Where perception is important for others to view an individual, what she stands for, and other moral considerations, what we use to "dress" the image that is portrayed relies heavily on effective scenery as a polioptic device. Choosing the correct color scheme, decorations, logos, lighting, etc. all culminates to an assurance that the leader or representative will be seen as providing the correct manner of expression and have an appropriate relationship between the groups he is trying to reach and the leader himself.

In an office setting, the make-up of wall space, desk, books on shelves, etc. all have a calculated measure that must be utilized to one's advantage and be considered an effective ally when navigating workplace politics. As an example, diplomas should be hung in a consistent pattern on walls and in similar, executive frames to solidify training and expertise in specific areas of the business or industry in question.

But it does not meet the polioptic litmus test to hang only one diploma on a wall. Rather, utilize the space as a timeline of distinction and visual resume of the educational value the individual brings to the company, district, agency, or corporation. In the same venue, the office area should include softer elements, such as plants and different types of family, sports, and historic memorabilia.

Books on shelves should reference several classic titles and important authors, researchers, analysts, etc. from the immediate field or industry. Reference texts and law books are always of quality and catch someone's "eye" where polioptics come into play. An individual's desk should appear to be "busy," but that is not to be confused with messy and disorganized. The perception must always be that an individual is always busy and working on something, but has that information under control.

SOCIAL MEDIA

The true beacon of polioptic persuasion and measures of perception to navigate workplace politics is the utilization of social media. Through its creation alone, social media provides an optical lens dedicated to getting messages to individuals in order to gain perspective on an individual topic or need. Information can be sent and received through numerous outlets and to a multitude of individuals who can unwrap the message in any way they see fit.

Social media can also provide different types of scenery, slogans, etc. while aligning groups with others to connect suitable partners in helping to promote engagement or denounce a proposal. Social media is constantly advancing and must be utilized by a leader to establish a good rapport with constituent groups and help get her "message" out to others. However, a cautionary tale holds true as well, in that certain sites and postings can bring with them negative referrals as well. One must be very careful when posting specific items, articles, or writings and report only information that can assist in moving the goal forward rather than negating all of the hard work that has been accomplished.

CHECKING FOR UNDERSTANDING

How Are You Perceived?

- What types of polioptics have you used when hosting an important event?
- What polioptical devices can hurt an aspiring leader? How can this be avoided?

Chapter 6

Using Perception to Navigate Workplace Politics

What is the recipe for putting theories into practice, ensuring that an effective leader is using perception to assist with the engaging of tasks; moving the mission forward; and motivating staff members? It is easy to read the concepts and gain knowledge of the subject to assist in the transition of any leader and leadership team; however, putting those theories into common practice to successfully motivate constituent and stakeholder groups can sometimes become a tricky task.

The first rule in navigating workplace politics is to "know" the actual workplace politics. Not so much what the "perceived" politics are but what holds true for your specific office, district, township, or organization. Experts in organizational leadership will argue that the political atmosphere of any organization is dictated by the powers in charge. Whether it is the CEO of a large corporation or the Board of a non-profit organization, the culture and climate of the workplace depends on the actions of the majority and the dissent of the minority members in the hierarchical scheme.

Successful managers and leaders of teams within the workplace understand the major "players" involved in the decision-making roles pertinent to the political components that make up the scope and structure of the leadership. To be successful, one must ensure that he is perceived as supporting each of the members in the majority hierarchy while still supporting those individuals considered in the minority. This can be an extremely cumbersome task, and it is not something that can be tackled immediately by a freshman leader or administrator.

Individual leaders who are successful in utilizing the art of perception to navigate workplace politics do so with an independent style that provides others with an awareness that the leader is in control and can carry out the mission of the business or organization. Leaders use perception through these different modalities to control a specific situation at hand; curry favor with specific stake-holders or constituent groups; establish specific parameters; and strengthen influencers to assist in moving the mission of the organization forward. In all, navigating the political aspects of the workplace is just as important as one's ability to perform the operations, scope, and duties of the job successfully.

TYPES OF PERCEPTION

The word perception comes from Latin (*percipio*) and is defined as the way of regarding, understanding, or interpreting something (Oxford English Dictionary). There are several types of perceptive devices that a leader can perform and perfect to help assist her in creating an environment that permits her to strategize and sustain adequate trends in the positive expansion of the goals and merits as established through her job description.

Along with other workplace-readiness tactics and skills, a leader can define her own outline of success while utilizing dialogue, examples, and past performance objectives to measure and execute the short- and long-range goals that align with the growth expectations she has set for both herself and others. To lead is to be perceived by one's own constituents as powerful within any organization.

Not power that is gained through physical means or a fear from inadequate job performance; rather, to be a true leader it must be perceived by all that the individual in question has a strong, firm handle on the daily operations and flow of the organization or office while understanding the human aspects of his workforce with an overwhelming appreciation for the pride in performance that it is revered for on a daily basis. For example, a manager who sends a quick note or email to her staff every few weeks, letting them know they are appreciated is perceived as taking the time to care and understand how hard each member of the team is working.

PERCEPTION FOR GAIN

To gain something means to obtain something desired or profitable. Using methods of perception and sensory awareness, a leader can gain power or confidence within a particular situation and help affect the outcome to a most favorable level. This method does not define a specific sensory device; rather, using sources of influence, praising others, identifying subordinates' concerns, and taking time to know your team of workers on a personal level are just some ways in which a leader could strengthen the power bond that continues to be perceived by others.

PERCEPTION TO FAVOR

To favor is to feel or show approval or preference for an individual person or an action that is directly related to an outcome specific to your leadership goals. This can be considered a "tricky" method in one's toolbox, in that, if it is perceived that you are favoring one individual over another, there may be additional consequences related to the decision that is made. With this, sometimes the perception of a leader favoring one position over another can work to his advantage.

Stakeholders and workers alike can work harder to ensure that the leader curries favor toward their own position, and the leader can use this part of workplace politics to promote production, strengthen workplace readiness skills, and demand more from his constituents.

The leader is cautioned to ensure favoring a single side doesn't potentially negate production from other facets of the company. Instead, it must be perceived that the entire team benefits from the advancement of each unit of the team.

PERCEPTION TO ESTABLISH

At times, a leader will need to establish a strong position on something that is consequential to the success of the company, organization, or a short-/long-term tenet of the institutional mission. When a leader uses her influencers to direct attention, production, supplies, budget, and marketing strategies to a particular position, it can be easily perceived that the need to ensure successful growth is established through the goals and actions of the administrative hierarchy.

Conversely, if it is the perception of subordinates or workers that there is a lack of interest by the managing team members, then productive measures may become lax, and weakened oversight may be detrimental to the overall organizational goals as prescribed by the leader. One must also use caution in not providing a false sense of excitement or act "phony" when trying to establish a position or the importance of a product or method.

Too often at times, being overzealous, quirky, or just not "oneself" can be perceived as "fake." This perception would be detrimental not only to the specific campaign described but also to the individual leader's/manager's character and care for concern throughout the company or organization. A leader cannot be faulted for establishing a strong excitement for creativity, influence, and sacrifice that her team makes to get to a level of productivity that is indicative of the organization's success; however, going too far by being overly persuasive, overfamiliar, and super-sensitive to the needs of constituents can backfire when perception must prevail.

PERCEPTION AS AN INFLUENCE

Overall, the art of perception in workplace politics will work to ensure a leader gains favor while establishing a position of positive production for the overall wellness and growth of a company or institution. In every industry or career field, the political structure is versed somewhat in leveraging the wants and desires of those individuals who have something that another individual needs.

What an individual can perceive as true can usually be achieved through the utilization of services, words, actions, and so on that influence the trajectory specific to the goal of the individual person or organization. Influencers as individuals are perceived by others to have more knowledge than others, or be better versed, in particular matters that help shape the landscape of a career field; the growth of a product; or add credibility to a brand or individual.

Perception as an influence can be evidenced through the amount of experience an individual has with regard to the topic and the success of the influence measured by the number of followers drawn to said measure. For example, a wise orator with over twenty years of experience in leading a successful company to Fortune 500 status will have thousands of potential candidates for positions and clients follow his organization, structure, and the decision-making models he uses to invoke strategies against market components in order to obtain optimal growth in a career industry. Why? Because he is perceived as being successful in his field, and he exudes enough influence over others who aspire to become him.

This type of influence continues to grow the perception of his power and strengthens his position within his competitive arena. On the other hand, someone perceived as minimally or not successful in his field will have little influence as the driving force behind the organizational structure, leading to diminished returns and a fractured following.

CHECKING FOR UNDERSTANDING

How Are You Perceived?

- Identify three ways that an individual can work to better understand workplace politics.
- What types of influencers can an individual use to grow the perception of power in an office, school, or business setting?
- Describe a way that you used perception to ensure that an individual favored a situation in which you were involved.

Chapter 7

Becoming Aware as a Leader

Too often, leaders are not aware of the systems of management that encompass their daily routines. In turn and in order to survive, they become managers facing transactional tasks instead of transforming an organization into a more global setting. Leaders must be aware of political motives and other perceived actions that can cause the mission to fracture and create problems for the individual leader.

Awareness is the knowledge or perception of a situation or a factual issue. A leader who is aware is perceived as having great concern about a particular situation and is well-informed about the development of the situation in question. There are several important areas of awareness that can be seen as instrumental in advancing an individual's popularity, respect, desirability, and propensity to lead. These awareness areas include self-confidence, self-motivation, and an ability to communicate with others.

SELF-CONFIDENCE

A strong leader has a high level of self-confidence in order to promote self-awareness while strengthening his role within the organization. To be self-confident is to trust in one's own abilities, qualities, and judgment in determining the best for the leader and his constituent base. Self-confidence is contagious, and a leader who is perceived as being confident in a group, mission, company, or product most always exudes those same qualities within himself since he supports his role in building success for the organization.

To have, or be perceived as having self-confidence will help an individual strengthen his chances of having subordinates and others follow his direction in a more prominent manner. In order to be self-confident, a leader must research and "know" a situation, product, program, etc. "inside-and-out." Although understanding the strengths of something is important, it is much more important to understand weaknesses and find alternate ways to help mitigate the potential losses that are connected to those weaknesses.

To expand on this, one of the most difficult assignments that anyone had to complete in high school was the personal essay. Sure, we can write volumes about or can stand in front of a room and introduce our best friend, but when it comes to describing ourselves, individuals usually have a difficult time putting the right words together to help assure others that they have the confidence to describe themselves to other individuals. "What could I say about myself that doesn't seem conceited or pompous?" or "What if I say something that makes me sound weak or frail?"

Now, consider the proverbial question that each of us will be asked in an interview for that perfect career position for which we have long awaited.

"So, that was great to hear about your strengths Jonny, but can you give me a few of your weaknesses?"

Suddenly, Jonny "freezes," and the interview comes to a halt.

"Uh . . . gee, um well I think a weakness is I work too hard sometimes?"

Wrong Jonny! It is a sign of strong self-confidence if Jonny can humble himself to engage in a conversation, especially in an attempt at first meeting someone, about a weakness that not only he has, but that he recognizes and can talk about as well. Everyone has weaknesses. That doesn't make an individual weak, it makes an individual human. And "being human" goes a very long way when one is hoping to be perceived by others in such a way to gain their support in a particular situation or in the workplace. Further, a leader or individual who is confident in facing her own weaknesses and attempts to work to fix them through self-motivation and an intense work ethic proves that she also has self-confidence in her ability to move the needle forward.

SELF-MOTIVATION

A leader must be perceived as having a strong work ethic and be a self-motivator in order to be assured that his team is performing in the same manner. Through leading by example, subordinates, workers, and colleagues understand that the goal of the mission is not too small or less important because the leader is also involved.

Although a leader most often will be too busy to involve herself in the specific or magnitude of details involved in each and every action of the organization and/or the task at hand, her direct involvement in specific areas of individual projects goes a very long way in consideration of production and growth. There is even more to be gained when a leader is perceived as completing a task that is not in the public eye or will be discussed in a public venue. Here, she shows that she is more motivated to advance the mission of the entire team, and each individual member of it, rather than just herself.

A leader or individual perceived as being self-motivated is one who inspires others in and around her to do the same thing. Soon, the group or organization will include full teams of individuals needing little supervision and more facilitating and/or coaching. Take as an example a major league sports team. Although at that level, individual athletes still work on perfecting the fundamentals of the game, one can argue that the player's fundamental skills have already risen to such an advanced level that she has met, or surpassed, the caliber of professional level standards.

Well if that's true, then what does a coaching staff do? The managerial and leadership teams of those professional sport organizations facilitate and strengthen the advancement of competition in consideration of those skills as compared to other organizations. However, without players who are self-motivated to continue to enhance their own skills, the group dynamic becomes flawed and unproductive. In the end, who will suffer the most? Make no mistake that the perception of failure always falls on those in charge.

CLIMATE CONSIDERATIONS

The first perceptive measure of pronouncing awareness that a leader can partake in is understanding the climate and surrounding environment of the workplace and workplace politics. As was discussed in earlier chapters, being savvy in and around the workplace and individuals in specific departments is extremely beneficial to assuring the leader has an idea of the "pulse" of the organization.

Not only is this important to the leader himself for his own benefit in consideration of his leadership role in the company, district, or department, but it is also important to his constituent base and the individual groups with whom he is in contact with. Each of these groups gives some type of benefit to the organization, and how that benefit is gained, lost, or perceived each way will wholly affect the culture and climate of the organization.

The leader needs to be aware of the strengths and weaknesses of the operations that surround the intake and output of her organization. Which individuals are in charge of specific systems, and who do those individuals report to? Which systems, which are already in place, aren't working properly, or which systems are missing? Is there enough support staff and equipment to ensure proper productivity, or is there something lacking? Even if the leader doesn't have all of the answers upfront, the ability to investigate workplace norms and separate the efficiencies from deficiencies in a timely manner helps subordinates and colleagues alike support the leader's role in the organization.

The ultimate "win" for any leader is moving the organization forward and having tangible results that can be recorded and reported as evidence that some growth has occurred. In order to decide the strategic planning and formulate actions specific to the needs of the actual organization, the leader must continue to be aware of nearly every aspect of the company, organization, building, or entity for which she is responsible. Awareness is a sense that forces others to perceive that the leader has an understanding and know-how to make things better, and the wherewithal to know what isn't working as well.

To fully understand the climate and landscape, an individual in his workplace must be attentive to the interactions around him, and he must note the alliances that are being made as well. It is just as important to ask the right questions and know when to listen instead of comment.

DESK AUDITS

Desk audits are an easy and efficient way for managers, leaders, and supervisory staff to ensure that systems are operable, efficient, and contain the appropriate expected data of the organization. Desk audits can be completed to verify employee records; reconcile budgets; check personnel fingerprint records; assure licenses and certifications are valid; etc. Basically, any system or function of a business or financial officer can be audited for compliance issues.

Performing such audits is evidence that a leader or supervisor is monitoring performance creating the perception that he is becoming aware or supporting the data he has received from both informal and formal observations. As others in the organization perceive this as a useful tool, the supervisor will have successfully acknowledged that he is involved with the intricacies of compliance and how he has a strong sense of urgency and strictness in the value of the ethical charge of the organization.

RESEARCH AND DEVELOPMENT

To continue to advance the mission of the organization through the enhancement of a product line, system, or a service can be perceived as one of the most important ingredients in growing a workplace, company, or organization. The only way to sharpen the competitive edge in consideration of the organizational values, mission, and vision that most likely "hangs" on the walls of the workplace office is to continue to understand the product or program and the market which will ultimately decide its success.

By surveying and asking questions of clients, constituent groups, etc., and researching the competition and how it handles fluctuations in market strategy, it can easily be perceived that there is an interest in the long-term sustainability of what is at stake, which tends to show others and subordinates how important their own investment is to the overall success of the organization.

WHO'S ON THE TEAM?

Another area where an individual's own perception of circumstances will help her navigate workplace politics is knowing "who" is on each "team." Through conversations, questioning, and the active art of listening for particular answers and cues, a strong or aspiring leader knows who, in both her inner circle and on the periphery, is in support of her needs and values and who is adverse.

In turn, knowing what the team makeup is will allow the individual to ensure that certain details aren't shared with particular members and, more importantly, which members to share specific information with. To offer an example, let's first identify a member of the office who has been observed to not be able to keep much information to himself. In other words, "he likes the tea." In most situations, valuable information, confidential matters, and issues dealing with personnel would be kept in strict confidence and away from this individual.

However, what if there is a particular statement or response to a situation, which definitely cannot be revealed by the manager or leader, that could be beneficial to the manager if the information did "leak" somehow? Simply put, knowing this characteristic need exists within a team member can be useful in the individual getting what she needs by sharing the information through appropriate means. A leader who is perceived as knowing her co-workers and subordinates is also perceived as understanding the dynamics of the team, the alliances that are established, and the strengths and weaknesses of all its members.

DANGERS OF AWARENESS

The biggest danger of having certain "awareness" in the workplace is that others can perceive specific actions as a weakness or misstep in determining positive outcomes for the organization, district, or company. As perception remains key in navigating workplace politics and advancing in the organization, realizing that being aware of your alliances and even being comfortable with his status in the team can cause an individual to let his guard down.

A leader must ensure that he is comfortable with everything that is occurring when imagining how an outcome should be perceived. If his "gut" feeling tells him something isn't "right," an investigation into the matter must ensue. In the workplace, a small problem can easily create a very large distraction. Always remember, it's not the 100-mile march that is so bothersome—it's the pebble in your shoe (Confucius).

CHECKING FOR UNDERSTANDING

How Are You Perceived?

• What is something that a leader can do to ensure her team consists of self-motivators?
• What are some protocols you follow to motivate yourself to complete a task?

Chapter 8

Modeling Your Skill Set

We all have strengths and weaknesses, and there is a particular skill set that has helped an individual become the strong leader he is today. It is important that the leader continues to model that skill set to his constituent groups to be perceived as relevant to the other members of the organization and those individuals who surround the team with the hope of elevating to a leadership role. Modeling not only shows subordinates how the mission should be accomplished but that you are highly proficient in consideration of the matter at hand.

In nearly every career field or industry, there is some type of internship, monitoring, or observation that a new worker to that position must partake in in order to be considered "ready" for that field or occupation. In the case of all licensing areas, there is a required number of hours and training modules that need to be successfully completed so that a transition to the field can be made successfully. This type of training or coaching comes in the form of a seasoned worker or a leader within that company, district, or labor industry.

It is here in these apprenticeship or intern scenarios that we see the best demonstration of modeling individual skill sets in a perceived relevance to success. As the intern, one takes for granted that the group, organization, or individual who is overseeing the training program and caused the mentor selection to occur has done an incredible amount of vetting of this "coach," and she is the most competent and experienced person to prepare others for their entrance into their new career or approval to receive their licensing and credentials.

Just the mentor or trainer being assigned creates enough perception that this individual is successful; knows how to provide the appropriate oversight to ensure another individual's success; and has enough experience in all facets of the field to ensure the individual knows how to handle any situation that comes his way. Here, we realize how trust and perception sometimes go hand in hand. This is important to understand as one utilizes perception to navigate the workplace and other areas of life where influence is necessary.

Where trust and perception are synonymous isn't always the truth, one must consistently question or become better informed of the forces that surround the connection at hand. Let's take for example a taxicab driver. So, when my oldest daughter first got her license, I knew her strengths and weaknesses behind the wheel because my wife and I had trained her over the course of a year prior to her turning seventeen. Since I knew her so well, I became uber-sensitive and overly cautious of the way she chose to perfect her driving capabilities. I wanted her to "slow down" at every curve, and I needed her to drive just like me.

Months following her receiving her standard license, I was still extremely reluctant to have others drive with her. Although I knew that I would be worrying about her on the road now for the rest of my life, I wasn't convinced that I should put others in the car with her. Even my other three children. However, she did pass all of the written and practical requirements, spent a multitude of hours "behind-the-wheel" with myself and professional driving instructors, and became a pretty attentive driver in her year of training. Regardless, I was still hesitant to accept the fact that my daughter was ready to drive me or others as safely as I could.

On the other hand, in New York City one blustery afternoon my wife and I decided to take a taxicab uptown to grab some lunch in Little Italy. Like a "pro," I stuck my handout to flag down a checkered cab to take us to our lunch date.

"Mulberry Street, please."

Who was this gentleman? Well, he obviously is a cab driver because he is driving a checkered cab. And he is obviously a great driver because "they" wouldn't give him his license if he wasn't. "Somebody" checks and tracks every cab driver's record and monitors them for reckless driving, speeding, and any accidents. So, who are "they" and who is "somebody"? Interestingly enough, the perception I have regarding the taxi driver being better than my daughter at driving comes with no vetting and absolutely no indication that I am right.

Rather, because I perceive this all to be so, I trust that there are others doing the right thing. At the same time, I already determined and had perceived that this driver was a safe and satisfactory driver long before I stepped into his cab just based on my eagerness to flag him down. If I didn't perceive that to be so, I would never have taken the taxicab.

We see this in all different industries and organizations around the globe. We trust that everyone is doing his or her own job so perfectly that there is little room for error when in fact, that condition is truly what makes perception reality. I remember being on a plane at seven years old clutching my father's leg just after takeoff. As the phenomena of flying will never cease to amaze me, as a young man I remember answering my father's concern.

"What are you doing?"

"I am afraid that the pilot will crash."

My father, relentlessly stoic, retorted without hesitation.

"What, you think the pilot wants to die too?"

Although most likely not a message from the father-of-the-year winner, it all made sense. If the pilot did his job, then he would be as safe as I was. It's the same reason why we each enjoy reasoning that an individual we are made to follow or emulate is the person who is absolutely "doing it the right way." In reality, after some time and thought about what is best for all constituents involved, we tend to come to the realization that not anyone can be right all the time. Regardless, it is that initial perception that we have about leaders and mentors that makes them omnipotent and a force to lead the rest of their subordinates, interns, and students toward the right way of doing things.

To accomplish this further, the leader must model what it is that he is perceived to be doing correctly so that his subordinates, etc. can understand how it should be done in order to ensure success. In doing so, not only does the perception of his leadership skills grow since he is modeling through example, but the leader is continuing to expand the tendrils of his base, providing a structure for longevity in the organization which will only help to strengthen the mission of the organization or company. This can be best evidenced and analyzed through the metamorphosis of large companies that can trace their origins back to single-room offices where one or two employees did everything from sales and marketing to production and shipping.

Through hard work and solid branding, the founders/owners pass on their own vision and philosophy to each member of their company that they hire, modeling what their expectation is for the continued production of the product or compliment of the service which they provide. Here, modeling the needs of the company allows others to feel what the leader knows to be right when determining the success of the company and/or brand as a whole. Through modeling, there is no contradiction or confusion as to what is expected by all other individuals within the organization.

CHECKING FOR UNDERSTANDING

How Are You Perceived?

- Name three occupations or industries where perception plays a definitive role in trusting individuals to perform their jobs successfully.

- Describe a time when you were an intern or mentored by a member of upper management/administration. What were some of the influential markers that the individual mentor made during your observations that you use today?

Chapter 9

Pride in Performance

Taking pride in each and every aspect of your performance will allow for a leader to be perceived as an extremely successful individual. Even those individual leaders who are struggling within different areas of their organization who hold their composure are only perceived to still be extremely effective, in control, and part of a successful business/organization of which others would wish to contribute or become more involved. Having pride in oneself is a trait that is necessary for success to be realized in nearly every aspect of an individual's personal and professional life. Without it, outside influences and poor decisions can plague relationships, productivity, and lessen self-worth.

Regardless of the activity, action, or relationship, pride is a formidable ingredient in any leadership recipe. Taking pride in every aspect of one's performance ensures that confidence and self-respect is given by members of a group on the basis of some distinctively shared identity and cultured experience. As it is important for any individual to use this trait as a healthy determinant to accepting the path that one has chosen in all aspects of his life, it must always be monitored closely. When pride suffers, so does an individual's ability to perform in all areas of business and livelihood, leaving others to perceive some sense of weakness in that individual which would most likely lead to a lack of confidence in his leadership abilities.

A leader must strengthen this trait in order to ensure that others perceive him as confident, daring, and able to handle their needs as well. Having pride, or lack thereof, in yourself or your organization is contagious and the effects usually stem from the roles of leaders within the organizational hierarchy. If pride in all aspects of performance is taken seriously by the chief officer, then all other members will understand the importance of the practical nature that acts as the foundation for successful performance in said organization, corporate, non-profit, or governmental structure.

The opposite, meaning that the chief is lax, unorganized, inattentive, or unaware of the needs of her subordinates or the organizational trends that are occurring, is detrimental to the infrastructure, culture, and climate of the organization. In turn, the lack of pride in oneself and the overall organization will lead to a breakdown of priorities; reduce trust in relationships within the organization; lessen the worth of both internal personnel and the perception of what the organization represents from the "outside looking in"; and cause any forward-leaning progress to halt and even bring detriment to the production of the organization as a whole.

Where do we recognize this lapse of pride most? Well, it is truly perceived in organizations and communities where the leadership seems guarded by this sense of "old power," where shaking the status quo can be seen by some as a weakness. The "don't rock the boat" mentality helps to cement the fact that pride can be seen as a stale trait, where with some individuals, growth seems to be a challenge when change should be inevitable. A true leader looking to navigate a workplace successfully and elevate through different positions must recognize the importance of performing in a positive direction, where moving the needle just a little is better than going backward.

Individuals of the mindset that when pride in oneself is perceived by others in the organization, it becomes contagious also know that power can be gained and influenced by involving all stakeholders in the growing of pride in the organization. For instance, in reviewing a company's mission statement, all company stakeholder groups must be represented in leading the charge behind the change or amended mission. By including feedback loops while involving all different and distinct program departments (and individuals from within those departments), the group works together to take onus for the productive outcomes that will now trigger a stronger and more unified performance.

As the power struggle in any organization, company, district, or team is very real, a person who utilizes measures that will indicate a favorable influence among specific individuals and, in turn program or personnel decisions, allows others to perceive that her input is not only respected but stems from a satisfaction derived from her own achievements and successes, along with the achievements of others, that replicate an ability to be proud of oneself and what has been accomplished.

These measures include, but are not limited to the enhancement of self-esteem, self-respect, a heightened self-worth, and management of individual ego. But how does one solidify the perception that he takes pride in everything he does? The answer is simple—he takes pride in everything he does! There is no secret to winning over a staff or team of subordinates when revisiting this topic.

Having pride in all a leader does and pride in herself only acts as an assurance that her entire team will have pride in what its mission is leading to better teamwork, sharper communication skills, and greater overall performance. Leading by example is the true method to enhancing any workplace, and in consideration of navigating the needs of individuals as well as one's own needs, putting theory into practice is truly the only method.

CHECKING FOR UNDERSTANDING

How Are You Perceived?

- Recall an instance in your professional career where you received satisfaction for the completion of a task or through reaching a milestone. How did your gratification enhance the pride you exemplified in consideration of your performance and drive for future goals?
- As a leader, what are some methods/ways in which you can help a colleague or subordinate advance his self-worth?

Chapter 10

Competitive Persuasion for Leaders

A major key in using perception to navigate the political aspect of leadership in the workplace is the ability to persuade others, using perceptive measures, to accomplish tasks and motivate subordinates. The competitive modifier is included because leaders are only effective when they win. Each and every decision must result in a positive outcome in order to be perceived as successful. Even a Pyrrhic victory is a true "win" if it is perceived in such a way.

So, what parts of perception gives the leader a true edge over the rest of the competition? Although the mode and methodology varies based on the situation at hand, using perceptive devices to persuade others to gain influence is an important lesson in navigating workplace politics. If the leader is perceived as knowing—then he is knowledgeable. If the leader is perceived as possessing "old power" as an influencer, then he will be viewed through a transactional lens.

If it is the perception of constituent groups that the leader of an organization or company values being transparent and she engages in analyzing feedback loops, then she is perceived as gaining "new power" and brings an awareness to the group that the value of their input is important to the success of the entire team. Using perception to persuade and influence should be viewed through a competitive mindset.

In other words, a true leader works to secure a competitive edge when assuring that her methods of persuasion are the sharpest tools in her toolbox. Whether it is the way she addresses others, her ability to lead people to making an informed decision, or changing the views of another individual through designed premeditated tactics, competitive persuasion is influential in garnering the support and functionality a leader needs to move toward defining and reaching the goals of the organization. In doing this, a leader can grow her leadership capital to levels that will greatly assist her with future strategic planning and exponentially advance trends in the organization, activities, and systematic flow of the workplace.

ENHANCING LEADERSHIP CAPITAL THROUGH PERCEPTION

While growing support for one's leadership style is influenced greatly by what a leader can produce for an organization or business, the art of perception and how the leader ensures she is viewed by others can greatly add to her leadership capital. Leadership capital is defined as a measure of the extent to which leaders and holders of positional power within a political environment can effectively attain and wield authority. Leadership capital consists of three leadership components: skills, relations, and reputation.

The notion of leadership capital describes the difference between being in charge and being in power.[1] When subordinates or other members of the company or organization can gauge the skills of a leader or manager and compare that to other members of the team, the competitive spirit of the workplace continues to flourish since the leader is encouraging growth in the workplace through competition.

For example, a sales manager who is in direct charge of a team of sales individuals can encourage, coax, and support his members into becoming the leading regional sales team utilizing relationships and his reputation of being a concerned and supportive leader throughout the entire process. However, his ability to spotlight his skill set and model how he can add to that competitive spirit forces others to increase the investment they each are making in the confidence they have in him to move the group forward.

BE THE ROOM

When you are responsible for facilitating a meeting or event, a leader must ensure that she is ultimately the "face" of the room. I know this sounds conceited in nature and not a measure of the "humbled" administrator, however the perception must be that you are in control of every aspect of the event that is taking place. It is further important that the individual ensures that she doesn't come across as a micromanager.

Rather, by delegating tasks in an appropriate manner and even allowing other members of the leadership team to introduce or emcee parts, if not all, of the program it will be perceived that she is in control of each and every aspect and outcome of the event. Is it extremely important that the leader remains visible and can be connected to every faction at the event, in some way or another? This is even more important if there is an individual, competitor, or even an "enemy" at the event where, as the leader assures that she is seen with these individuals, she maintains a collective cover with regard to her true feelings about others in the room.

USE NAMES

It is extremely imperative that a leader, or aspiring leader, uses names when addressing others at in-person meetings and events. Ensuring that this is something that can be done almost at all times is an easy way to get the competitive edge that one seeks when looking to persuade others in business and in order to be perceived as that leader who really takes an interest in the personal and professional lives of others.

I know this sounds simple, but as power grows exponentially and months turn into years of different leadership roles, so does the number of contacts and friends of contacts who the leader is expected to know. Of course, a majority of the names of acquaintances, partners, vendors, and the like will be remembered. However, it is that modest set of individual stakeholder, employees, etc. that somehow seemingly slips our memories.

There are several tactics that can be utilized in order to ensure that one can communicate with others through a proper greeting. Alone, the individual could be briefed by his team in knowing who will be attending the event. As names are reviewed, he would be able to pinpoint who would or would not be recognizable to him during the event. This could lead to further preparation and review of the program and protocols that will be addressed that evening.

Using a "partner" to assist in remembering names is the better tactic. This can be an assistant who makes the introduction first, "Oh you remember Michael, right?" or a significant other who takes the lead after a signal is given. My wife is incredible at this "trick," knowing when we are at a function that if I don't immediately introduce her to a guest with whom I engage in conversation with, she will extend her arm as a welcome gesture and lead with, "Hi, I am Jaimie, Rich's wife."

Although it may be perceived as "rude" that I did not introduce my wife to a colleague or guest, I always acquiesce by replying, "Oh, I'm so sorry, yes this is my wife." However, that apology only comes after the guest has already returned the greeting to my wife and I hear the guest's name. A very simple tactic that becomes important throughout the remainder of the night as it becomes easier now to engage and include that specific guest in conversation instead of trying to avoid him because I can't remember his name.

RESEARCH TOPICS

It is crucial that one knows everything about a topic being discussed prior to discussing the topic. Well, maybe not everything—but definitely several major talking points and a good handle on the facts and abstract. Even though the leader may not be an expert in the topic, it can easily be perceived that she is knowledgeable as long as she knows more about the topic, and communicates the pros and cons with regard to the key issues at hand, than anyone else in the room. This is especially true when dealing with metrics and facts based on specific production of the office or organization.

If she is going to praise her team members for an increase in profit margins from last year, then she must know what the increase is. Talking points that include facts, individuals, successes, and failures help capture the true essence of the topic, and it allows for further discussion to be facilitated as well. The more input and research that is given, the more dialogue is fostered which leads to a heightened sense of competence in the problem set forth. By providing evidence that she is knowledgeable on all matters of relevance to the cause, the leader makes sure that her constituent base perceives her as all-knowing on the topic, intensifying her support and enticing others to follow her command.

KNOW THE AUDIENCE

Where we "know" an audience, one has an innate distinction of controlling what that audience does. It is critical that a leader knows what the "make-up" of her room is and with whom she is speaking. Prior to any event or meeting, she should have a mental listing of all topics that need to be covered and discussed with regard to moving an agenda forward. It is just as important for her to know when and if to ask questions or establish an open forum. In most instances, an open-ended session somewhere within the meeting or program so the audience can participate provides the leader with an immediate feedback loop or a "check" for understanding on a topic.

This is obviously an important measure to use in order to be perceived as a good listener and taking the needs of the workplace environment into consideration. However, the leader must be careful that an inflexible feedback loop and schedule does not allow others to perceive that she is not the person she purports to be. It is indicative of good leadership and an influential manner of navigating the workplace and any political fodder that engulfs it through exceptional communication skills.

Knowing one's audience forces successful communication, more specifically in knowing more what not to say or do than what to say or do. Further, it is indicative of successful management and leadership to utilize other members of the team to assist her in outlining who exactly is "in" the audience. What are the tendencies of the room in consideration of the social, political, and work environment of the office? What are some of the major issues facing production and morale? What are some of the outliers that may come up during the meeting or program that can be addressed prior to any question or dissent from the crowd?

ANTICIPATE PROBLEMS

Anticipating dissent and any other problems that may arise is an effective method of dealing with internal issues and being able to direct the outcomes of those issues to one's benefit. Anticipation of this nature starts with the ability to acquire an incredible set of intelligence (intel) from other members of any organizational team or loyal subordinates always looking to earn "points" with the manager or leader.

The next important steps in the process are to organize answers to the problems at hand, and to know when to utilize those answers to deflect any negativity in the workplace or office. The most effective method is to set forth a "preemptive strike" based upon the question or situation that is ultimately designed to "trip the leader" in the first place. Let's say that your ally in the office comes to you and explains that others in the warehouse are "on edge" because they believe that they need additional training on a new software package installed last week.

You further uncover that the initial training period was not enough, and several people had to leave early due to a large emergency shipment of widgets that had to be processed and immediately shipped. With "intel" this specific, a leader must first ensure to protect his source by generalizing comments relative to the concern but acknowledging the concern overall. Also, this needs to be done prior to the question being asked or a comment on the problem being made to give the perception that he ultimately has the true pulse of the workplace and continues to understand, analyze, and accommodate the needs of his workers as well as himself.

By showing this greater cause for concern in a proactive way rather than responding in a reactive way, the leader tends to be seen as more relevant and aware of the culture and climate of the organization, company, or district rather than always putting out fires. Thus, in this case, he begins his meeting with acknowledging the incredible work that the team has engaged in and its accomplishments since the last meeting, and then moves directly into the problem.

"Well I was reviewing our implementation of the new software program just the other day, and I have noticed how hard all of you were working on some of the new modules that really will help us track production, but seem a little more complicated than the last program."

The group grows more intent, some shaking their heads up-and-down in a manner of agreement.

"We also had some of you leave that training because of the emergency order, and - I really appreciate you for that but, well it definitely cut into that training time."

The group now anxious, waits for you to finish.

"So, I have scheduled some additional training for all of us so we can really be comfortable with this software, and it will make our jobs much easier."

Here, the leader has solved the issue prior to any acknowledgment of it from the subordinate tree; has offered a solution to solving the problem; and has given praise and recognition for the work that has already been done. Further, the leader's purposeful placement of himself in the training causes the entire team to perceive how teamwork to the leader and, in turn, the organization is just as, or almost more, important than the production output itself. Sometimes, it's not always where you are going that created the greatest memory, but how you get there.

NEVER SAY "I DON'T KNOW" OR "NO COMMENT"

It will definitely happen. At some point when elevating through the chairs of leadership or management, something won't go the way it should. And then, the media outlets will grab hold of the conflict or crisis and plan to report on it. What's the worst thing a leader can do? Easy. Respond with "No comment."

The same holds true when the individual is asked a question by someone in an audience, group, or crowd in consideration of a topic that she may not know the answer to. "I don't know" is never a statement that would be perceived as "good" for a leader. The true perception of successful leadership relies on the ideal that the leader has the pulse of her organization and knows everything that is happening at all times. Obviously, that's not a possible feat to master. However, what can be mastered is the perception that she does.

For any situation where questions such as these arise, a rehearsed but heartfelt statement should immediately flow from her vernacular. "I understand that this is a difficult time for everyone here in our family, and I continue to look into this matter with my team and will act accordingly. We will keep everyone abreast of our findings." Even if she has no idea what has occurred, this statement gives every stakeholder and onlooker the sense that she is in control and has some sort of awareness of what needs to be investigated. Further, it proves that regardless of the outcome, there is a handle on the issue and further updates and communication will be provided.

TRY NOT TO "READ" YOUR SPEECH

Individuals prepare speeches and lectures and read off of their notes because they are afraid that they are going to forget something or get too nervous and not be able to address a crowd regardless of makeup or size. In spite of all of the anxiety that one must overcome when introducing public speaking into his leadership repertoire, being able to communicate the spoken work to others in a forum is an art form in and of itself. However, an individual receives more recognition, respect, and engagement when he "speaks" from the heart when addressing others, rather than needing to write down the words to do it.

The fear of stumbling or forgetting something is real—not only is it a "real" fear but it portrays "real" and raw emotion. Inflections, pauses, and the like are what keep one's audience engaged and receptive throughout a speech, over dialogue, or at a rally. Great orators memorize parts of speeches, and they are so well-versed in the subject they are professing that the dialogue becomes easy conversation between the group and themselves. It is remaining calm and confident that allows for others to appreciate a speaker's actions and motives.

Conversely, reading a speech narrows the receptive and forgivable methods of reasoning. The words become rehearsed, and the audience subconsciously knows that the speech was analyzed, tweaked, and reviewed more than once by the author/orator. Making a pronunciation mistake, stumbling, or even losing one's place can raise the perception that the individual is not as bright or prepared as she has previously portrayed and may be nervous.

The mispronunciation of a word could unleash a devastating blow as to the strength of the individual's leadership abilities. Further, some types of canned responses would not be viewed too favorably in consideration of the contribution and support that the individual feels about the topic, groups, company, students, etc. To be frank, if the leader reads a speech and stumbles over the words that she herself had written down, the negative result and perception of the audience with regard to her dedication, drive, and just plain intellect would be suspect.

BE PERSONABLE

A leader should not be perceived as being friends with co-workers or subordinates, but rather she should be perceived as being friendly and personable. The basic premise holds true in stating that she should treat others as she would want to be treated. This is an extremely important element when deciding that keeping people safe, physically and emotionally, should help lay the foundational building blocks in the pyramidal hierarchy that identifies the different areas of successful leadership in any workplace.

Allowing others to have the perception of her that she is also human, compels them to have empathy for her and act on it when she needs them as well. This may not only be due to a personal need, death in the family, or other social dilemma, but may also be due to some type of controversy or dispute in the office, or when she really needs their support in a business or managerial sense.

DIRECTED INFORMATIONAL LEADERSHIP

The ultimate form of competitive persuasion in leadership through perception is what is known as directed informational leadership. Here, the leader includes all stakeholder groups and factions in all areas of a decision-making process. From designing an outline or flowchart in steps to formulating a decision; creating strategies to advance the goal or mission; and collecting and analyzing data, members of the organizational team take part in the very process that will be agreed upon and used to make an informed decision.

At the end of this process, all constituent groups are represented and have a "say" in the outcome, and time was invested to ensure that all ideas, concerns, etc. were considered in creating a path to the best decision for the company, district, or team. Throughout the entire process, the leader encourages his team to review and analyze multiple pathways, ensuring a realistic and in-depth vetting occurs in order to have the ability to redirect any adverse support of a controversial decision to the process that had taken place.

In the end, the leader will make the ultimate decision based on several choices that had "floated to the top" after he had assisted in establishing the who, how, and why of what had to be decided. Hence, when the leader chooses the same answer, applicant, product, etc. that has been decided by the team, it should have been his choice all along, giving the perception now that he only reached that decision with the input, advice, and direction from the stakeholders involved.

DON'T BE A MICROMANAGER

Micromanager is probably one of the worst nouns that could be in a leadership vernacular. In fact, although some skills/tasks must be micromanaged at times, to be a micromanager is having one foot already out in the parking lot. A leader who is micromanaging her team is perceived as untrusting, overpowering, and unwilling to facilitate a workload.

Most members of the workplace thrive on becoming empowered to lead and complete tasks on their own and in their own manner. A leader should manage the stream of the workload and ensure that it follows the mission of the organization, but actually involving herself in the day-to-day operations of the project and all of the initial decisions that are needed to make the mission whole will one day cause the morale of the organization to be deflated while conflating a number of social and economic issues for the office as well.

LET OTHERS THINK THEY KNOW MORE THAN YOU

This is difficult for some aspiring and less seasoned leaders to handle, but giving the sense that others in the "room" know more about a subject, topic, or condition than a leader himself does can sometimes work to his advantage. Think of it as an outsider looking inside on a situation or topic. By taking a step back, he is in a better position to move things around and direct the conversation and decision-making from the periphery.

This is not easy for the individual who needs to be the center of attention or in charge of everything. As this is an advanced tactic in leadership persuasion, one must be cautious in navigating others who are taking control. However, at times, when an individual thinks she knows more than others, she immediately lets her guard down and ensures a greater leadership or "expert" responsibility.

This can work to the leader's advantage since he can expect more productivity out of her and his team while still showing others that he is in charge for a reason. This feat is accomplished by ensuring that he is still connected to the project or decision at the very beginning, intermittently throughout the process, and then again at the end.

LET OTHERS HELP LEAD

Being a facilitator is crucial to navigating the workplace and maintaining successful leadership while having a high acceptance rating from your subordinates. Convincing others to have an opportunity to help lead the organization, company, or mission is an incredible way to model the tenets of the workplace while helping to influence others in their own career paths, a sort of "giving back" to the field. Placing onus and responsibility on workers also enhances the sense of pride in the action and strengthens the overall brand awareness that a leader struggles to promote internally on a daily basis. Everyone wants to be "a boss" at some point.

When an individual knows that she is able to make decisions that will affect an outcome while still having the safety net to make mistakes since there is still oversight, the conditions are set to grow productivity and excite creative ideas. We see this more often than not when a project sets off a tangent project to relate to the core components of the original idea or action.

The ancillary project will add depth and advancement to the original thought, and where it stems from a subordinate who can lead that new goal through to its final stages, the results will be rewarding in consideration of several different metrics including human capital, resources, and production. Further, this type of creativity and action can become aggressively contagious, causing an outpouring of revitalized spirit in a team over the needs of production.

"POLITRICKS"

In the political arena, perception is the purest art form of all. It doesn't matter whether it is government politics in consideration of an elected office; workplace politics that occurs in every single job field; or politics within a local community sports booster club—it is important to understand that a person's perception of how a leader reacts to a certain situation is the first sign of reality.

When one can successfully express the need for a particular position by showing an understanding for the motive and need for others, one positions himself with a leverage that can be used to effectuate a change on his behalf. "Politricks" can be defined as using and caring for the needs of others to advance one's own individual agenda.

NEVER LET THE CROWD CONTROL
THE MICROPHONE

Never let the crown control the microphone. Period. This is arguably one of the most important rules for a leader during a presentation when concentrating on the importance of how any audience perceives how the meeting or event is unfolding, especially in larger crowds. The importance of "holding" the microphone is similar to the imagery of the conch shell in Golding's classic *The Lord of the Flies*. The rule of order for the young tribe was that you can only speak if you were holding the conch shell.

The shell, symbolic for power and influence over that moment in time, was passed around so that everyone can have his own say in the happenings of the day. The same holds true for the moderator within an assembled crowd. Not only does the perception of the strength of his role diminish, but a controversial topic can adversely "swing" the climate of the group against his favor. Further, sometimes it is difficult to remove the microphone from an individual impassioned about a topic.

By engaging an individual asking a question, the moderator has the ability to then frame the question to be perceived in such a way that may benefit him or his organization more. As he listens to the question, he would then be able to rephrase it in a particular context that would make it more palatable than the way it was delivered. Repeating what was asked for the entire crowd, in the way he wants it repeated, provides not only a clear path to the question but also an assurance that the question can be perceived in a certain way.

This is most important when ensuring that one has an answer for the critical and controversial questions being asked. The exact answer that the moderator wants to convey to the crowd can now be shared in the most beneficial manner to the moderator hosting the meeting.

This is not to say that someone should be silenced. That is totally different than a leader controlling the "crowd," and knowing what will be asked and when it will be asked as well. Therefore, a leader must be cautious to ensure that he is not perceived as attempting to stifle or drown-out some advancing question. Instead, he should solicit questions and then be able to phrase them in such a manner that meets the answer he needs to portray to his audience. At times, individuals who have the spotlight intend to change the landscape and can hurt communications. Further, how does a leader retrieve the physical microphone if an individual doesn't want to give it back?

BEING POLITICAL VS. BEING POLITICALLY SAVVY

A leader or aspiring leader can only successfully navigate workplace politics if she is perceived to be politically savvy rather than plain political. There is a sweeping difference between the two terms, and each holds distinct positives and negatives when considering different scenarios in which they are defined.

In general, being perceived as politically savvy is when an individual understands the political affiliations and relationships that occur in and around the workplace. For example, a savvy individual can identify board members, and understands how to interact accordingly. She also knows that when a board member is present in an office or has communication with the individual, she must let her superiors know the substance of this visit or conversation. In basic terms, being politically savvy is having a strong understanding of what is or is not important to the "running" of the business or organization, and how to act toward specific individuals and events that involve entities who have the authority to make decisions that will affect the overall operations of the organization.

On the other hand, being political is knowing these entities and then working for or against them by verbal, written, or physical means to ensure some specific outcome for a need or an event. Hiring a receptionist that is the best friend of a board member's spouse is considered a politically motivated action which means the leader is being political. In fact, there is very little "grey" in consideration of political "moves."

However, the unfortunate consideration is that motivation can become blurred when the traits of individuals are overlooked because of political connections. Remember that receptionist? Well, he could be the best spreadsheet creator and memorandum writer in the candidate pool; however, since he has a connection to the board member, all of that falls secondary.

What about actions that seem both politically savvy and political at the same time? More times than fewer, instances that include several entities can come across as such. Buying tickets to a fundraising dinner that the wife of your boss is sponsoring for Breast Cancer Awareness can be seen as being savvy and political. First, you are savvy to show that you care about an important cause, strongly believe in the cause, and are contributing to something that will benefit others. Since it is your boss's wife's event, it can be seen as political since others may caution that your donation to the cause could be given in so many alternate ways.

READ THE LOCAL PAPER

The best way to be perceived as a successful navigator of the workplace and its politics is by keeping up with the local happenings and news events in the area. This becomes even more important in specific service industries that rely on monies and support from the public. To have the pulse of the community and knowledge base to understand what the needs of the local culture and climate are is helpful to ensuring that pathways to success and positive interactions are obtained and sustainable.

CHECKING FOR UNDERSTANDING

How Are You Perceived?

- What do you feel is your strength when acknowledging the importance of competitive persuasion as a leader? What is a weakness?
- What other methods can be utilized to ensure one maintains the ability to control any situation or an audience?

NOTE

1. Bennister, M., Hart, P. and Worthy, B. Leadership Capital: Measuring the Dynamics of Leadership (December 15, 2013).

Chapter 11

Diction in Leadership

Improving a leader's diction, grammar, and syntax is a true perceptive measure that can influence others when making decisions. A higher order vocabulary forces a client, subordinate, colleague, constituent, etc. to perceive that you have the intellect and knowledge to operate a successful organization. It is imperative that a leader utilizes the appropriate concepts and proper level of communication in order to ensure that others will respect her level of competency. This is something that every leader and aspiring leader can practice so that the utilization of sentence patterns and definitions become a staple in her repertoire.

As a matter of caution, the individual should be extremely careful not to overuse a particular term which would tend not to "fit" every situation. When this occurs, the dialogue and purpose seem typically "fake," and the perception of an intellectual style turns to one of fraud. Nothing can be worse for a leader's image or stability in the workplace than his being seen as attempting to look smarter than he is. The utilization of a higher order vernacular in conversations and written concepts must flow smoothly and seamlessly.

The following chart (table 11.1) depicts a column of a sampling of simple words or statements that may be used in consideration of an organizational acumen for leaders. The first column includes a word choice that may be common to a somewhat relaxed leadership style, utilized as the leader is looking to make a point or carry out a conversation with a business partner, subordinate, potential client, or another individual she has engaged. The *Choice Diction* column refers to an alternate word that represents a more impressive word choice and would ensure that others perceive you to have a greater handle on the English language and are more professional when dealing with constituents and peers.

Table 11.1 Simple Words or Statements

Simple Word/Statement	Choice Diction	Definition	Notes
Over and over	Ad nauseam	Something repeated	
This is real	Bona fide	For real	
Around	Circa	Around	
Therefore	Ergo	Therefore; thus	
By itself	Per se	By or in itself	
If you do this for me . . .	Quid pro quo	This for that	
Very skillful	Adept	Having knowledge or skill	
Opposed	Adversarial	Relating to a hostile situation or an opposition	
Looks good	Aesthetic	As of beauty or how something is pleasant or unpleasant	
Not sure	Ambivalent	Uncertain; in-between two or more options	
Awesome	Anomaly	Something outside what is normal	
Tough	Assert	Declare strongly	
Likes	Avid	Genuine interest	
Honest	Candor	A trait of being honest; frank	
Same time	Coincide	Same time	
Satisfied	Complacent	Satisfied	
This works	Conducive	Make suitable	
I think . . .	Contend	Assert opinion for something	
Evidence shows	Corroborate	To back; with evidence	
In the end	Culminate	Final	
Put stuff together	Cultivate	Fostered growth	
I have respect	Deference	Respect for; to regard	
I protest	Demur	Go against; objection	
Terrible	Dire	Fearful	
Conflict	Discord	Disagreement	
Disrespect	Disdain	Lacking Respect	
Concern	Dismay	Hopeless; to be surprised	
Belittle; downplay	Disparage	To speak "down" to; degrade	
Not clear	Dubious	Questionable	
Irregular	Eccentric	Odd; Peculiar	
Horrible	Egregious	Very bad; poor act	
Let go	Emit	To release	
Emphasize	Emphatic	To emphasize something	
Last long	Endure	Withstand	
Changing constantly	Erratic	Deviate from the norm	
Bring out	Evoke	To draw out	
Aggravate	Exacerbate	Make more severe	

(Continued)

Table 11.1 Simple Words or Statements (*Continued*)

Simple Word/Statement	Choice Diction	Definition	Notes
Apply	Exert	To make an effort	
Spend	Expend	To use up	
Take advantage of	Exploit	To use someone or something for some type of profit or gain	
Mean	Ferocity	Toughness; vicious	
Do well	Flourish	Prosper	
Easy; simple	Fundamental	Basic	
What may happen is . . .	Hypothetical	Supposed event	
Embarrass	Ignominious	Humiliating; public shame	
Relay	Impart	To send or disclose; make known	
Careless	Imprudent	Not caring for consequence	
Start	Incite	To encourage	
I don't care	Indifference	To be detached from something	
Satisfy	Indulge	To satisfy	
Guess	Infer	To deduce or conclude something	
Uncontrollable	Insatiable	Difficult to satisfy	
I call for . . .	Invoke	To call or cause to be carried out	
I feel bad about . . .	Lament	To feel sorrow for	
A lot of money	Lucrative	Of much profit/money	
Mean	Malicious	To be spiteful	
To change	Malleable	To mold	
Small	Modest	Humble	
Change	Modify	To alter something	
Something new	Novel	New	
Specific	Nuance	A subtle difference in the meaning of something	
Cancel	Null	Void or ineffective	
He knows it all	Omnipotent	All knowing or powerful	
Suggest	Opine	To give opinion	
Get out	Oust	To remove	
Very important	Paramount	Superior	
Temper	Petulant	Irritable	
The top	Pinnacle	At the highest level	
It is likely that . . .	Plausible	Reasonable	
I want to make known . . .	Postulate	To assert or make known	
Very strong	Potent	Having much influence	
Useful	Pragmatic	Useful; something that is practical	
I would like to state . . .	Promulgate	To formally declare	

(*Continued*)

Table 11.1   Simple Words or Statements (*Continued*)

Simple Word/Statement	Choice Diction	Definition	Notes
I reject . . .	Refute	To prove something as untrue	
Give up	Renounce	To give up	
Reprimand	Reproach	To criticize	
I deny . . .	Repudiate	To refuse to believe as true fact	
I am smart at . . .	Savvy	Having practical intelligence or knowledge	
I'm very careful not . . .	Scrupulous	To pay attention too intensely	
Look into	Scrutinize	To examine carefully	
Drive me crazy	Spur	To incite	
Simple	Stark	Very plain	
The same . . .	Static	Unchanged	
Someone I manage	Subordinate	Someone lower in rank; to make someone dependent upon another	
After this . . .	Subsequently	Happening after	
To prove this . . .	Substantiate	To strengthen with evidence or data	
Difficult	Subtle	Hard to analyze	
Not nice	Surly	Unfriendly	
I am sensitive in . . .	Tactful	To be skilled in dealing with others	
It is temporary . . .	Tentative	Not final	
I told you everything . . .	Transparent	Truthful and open	
This is dangerous . . .	Treacherous	Dangerous	
I am all-over . . .	Ubiquitous	Being everywhere at once	
The same side . . .	Unilateral	On one side	
Never happened before . . .	Unprecedented	Historic in a sense; new	
Make sure	Validate	To prove	
To justify . . .	Warrant	To prove to be reasonable	
How much product . . .	Yield	An amount that is produced	
How much is it . . .	Appraise	To assess the quality of	
How bad is it . . .	Critique	To analyze something	
How many will we need . . .	Predict	To estimate or guess that something will occur	
Put these together . . .	Integrate	Combine together	
Make changes . . .	Transform	To change	
This will take the place of that . . .	Assimilate	To absorb something; integrate	
Let's develop something . . .	Cultivate	To develop	

(*Continued*)

Table 11.1 Simple Words or Statements (*Continued*)

Simple Word/Statement	Choice Diction	Definition	Notes
Let's arrange something...	Orchestrate	To arrange something	
This is a new procedure . . .	Innovate	To change through new methodology	
She is what a boss should be . . .	Epitome	Something that resembles a perfect type	
I accepted this calmly . . .	Equanimity	Calmness; composure	
Very meticulous	Fastidious	Concerned about detail	
Beautiful	Idyllic	Peaceful or picturesque	
Shrewd	Machiavellian	Cunning; scheming (in politics)	
I said it over and over . . .	Mantra	A repeated statement or slogan	
Very showy . . .	Ostentatious	Pretentious display; make notice	
Lazy	Perfunctory	A gesture carries out with minimal effort	
Mature	Precocious	Of certain abilities in a child that develop earlier than in other children	
It is a typical . . .	Quintessential	Typical example of something	
Continue to talk about . . .	Rhetoric	The art of effective persuasion in consideration of speaking or writing	
Overexcited	Zealous	Showing great enthusiasm	
This is abnormal . . .	Anomaly	Something outside of the standard or norm	
I questioned his correctness . . .	Propriety	The condition of being right or appropriate.	
The best	Exemplary	The best of its kind.	

CHECKING FOR UNDERSTANDING

How Are You Perceived?

- How would you rate how you converse with others in the workplace?
- What strategies can you use to help strengthen your use of diction that can enhance how you are perceived professionally by others?

Chapter 12

Every Day Is an Interview

An individual who is looking to navigate the political atmosphere of any business or industry and elevate to certain positions within the leadership hierarchy must understand that every work day, every decision, and every alliance is being measured in consideration of the vision of the organization or business. Those individuals charged with making promotional decisions are evaluating every move a leader makes. The perception of how that leader prepares to be part of that elevated role is critical to a successful outcome in consideration of any promotional opportunities in the workplace.

Here, perception is key. To navigate the workplace politics properly in order to achieve the goal of attaining a promotion or a particular position in the company, district, or organization, one must be perceived as having the know-how, intellect, and status to handle the position in question. Hence, he lives in a "fishbowl" as others continue to make judgments and tally mental votes on whether or not he is ready to make the leap to a leadership role.

By dealing with situations and expectations on a daily basis, every day becomes an interview. Unlike a candidate from "outside" the company or organization's walls where she stands on the perception of a resume, record, references, and social media traffic, an internal member of the team looking for elevation to a new role is in the spotlight every day. This can be seen as an incredible opportunity, or can be the demise of an individual.

When coming from the outside as a candidate, most potential subordinate workers will know nothing of the external candidate's past decisions or performance. Sure, there will be rumors and what a "friend heard from a friend," but the candidate comes to the organization with a clean slate. The only thing the subordinate groups perceive is that he must be the most qualified candidate in the whole pool and definitely what management is looking for in its next leader.

As an internal candidate, the past may follow the candidate throughout the selection process, forcing her to explain actions and interactions from the past and facing animosity from workplace competitors. It is important for her to get "in front" of these possible conditions and anticipate any political influences or hurdles that may complicate matters in her elevation to managerial and leadership positions.

Regardless, as an internal candidate (or if someone can be used as a reference who will be with the candidate on a daily basis), there are several daily "tests" that the individual will need to partake in in order to pass the litmus test of being management material. Unfortunately, one mishap on any given day can further thwart her ability to become the final selection.

However, her ability to understand and identify the mistakes she has made and her awareness in how to communicate the way in which she corrected said issue will help her be perceived as ready for the position. There are several questions that will drive the "tests" that the internal candidate will need to perform for on a daily basis making every day an interview.

DOES THE CANDIDATE LOOK THE PART?

Does the candidate dress for success? As a leader must lead by example, an office dress code or policy is a definitive measure of the culture and pulse of the company. As an internal candidate, what was his feeling on the dress code prior to his looking for this promotion? Is he well-kempt, giving the appearance of an executive ready to lead the mission and vision of the company or organization?

Although a person's individual style is that of her own and something that must be expressed as she has the right to do so, the reality lies within the parameters that certain "looks" or cultural "fads" may not be considered acceptable and may hinder the overall selection process. As a society, we may not agree with that but unfortunately, it is a stern reality. Especially in a conservative space, the addition of piercings, visible tattoos, etc. can cause someone to lose the confidence of others because of the perception from his style. Is that right? Of course not. And in some if not most cases, that type of discrimination is not legal.

However, there tends to be culturally embedded bias's as we relate individuals to performing in specific roles. Even though these actions do not change the intellect, drive, or performance of an individual, a candidate's look and impression is most definitely an influencer when deciding on a candidate for a management or leadership position.

In consideration of the everyday interview, an individual who can show that she is growing into her expected role can win over others through this type of impression. In stating this, however, the candidate must be careful not to change overnight, and transition slowly into this office-style metamorphosis. A drastic change too quickly can signal being fake which will create the perception that she will do anything to make the boss, board, CEO, etc. happy.

IS THE CANDIDATE ORGANIZED?

An internal candidate, who has her "stuff" together, will be perceived by others as an individual who will be able to organize an office or company in several different areas and in several different ways. This doesn't only have to be physical space. An organized prospective leader successfully ensures that he can organize his appointments, schedules, and contacts while being able to assist others around the office with their individual and group tasks as needed.

A clean desk should not equate to an "empty" desk. Individuals without work on their desktop or papers organized in some fashion can be perceived as not being connected to the mission or very productive. An individual should have an organized system of inbox and outbox items, memorandum stacking, and other business documents scattered appropriately about her desk.

Also, she must be careful to organize her belongings appropriately as well. Pictures of family and friends, sayings, and the like must be carefully thought of and reflect the office environment. Even books that sit on shelves must be chosen and placed in a particular manner to reflect the culture and scope of the office and department.

IS THE CANDIDATE THE LAST ONE
IN AND THE FIRST ONE OUT?

Everyone knows the worker who runs everyone else over to get out of the door at 5pm sharp. We also can point out the Monday morning person who "sneaks in" late during football season, disheveled and still half asleep. These are not the biographies of successful candidates. The individual who fares well on an everyday interview is that person who is early to work and finishes when his work is completed for the day. Now, that doesn't mean that he needs to pull an "all-nighter," however, he shouldn't be the first one lined up to get to the parking lot.

It suffices to say that elevation to a managerial or leadership position brings with it an increase in workload and time on task. In many career fields, this also increases the physical amount of time one spends in an office, at outside events, or when answering to the needs of his constituent and subordinate groups. The candidate cannot be perceived as the last one to enter in the morning and the first one out the office door when he is anticipating to be the model for others. This will be a major complication and can draw shade to his commitment to the task at hand and the company or organization as a whole.

DOES THE CANDIDATE KNOW THE ROLE?

When one discusses competency in leadership, she must understand the role of the position and what it entails to be successful for both the leader herself and her entire group. Does she know everything about the department or industry she is hoping to lead, and does she know how to be perceived as a great leader? Does she understand that being an incredible listener and a person with an innate ability to utilize the experiences of other members on her team to push the mission forward is the only way she can expand her role?

A candidate with expertise in the area or field and an educated competency gives evidence that she is ready to lead the team. It becomes even more impressive if she has gained such a level of competency systematically over her time within the office, allowing her to utilize the process of attaining that expertise as a leader to help others attain the same level of competency themselves. In other words, if she is successful in doing it that way and I learn it from her, I too will be successful.

Knowing the role and reaching a certain level of competency doesn't always necessitate earning some type of continuing education or a degree in a particular field. Rather, practical and life experience with the component, role, product, or service many times is the best foundation in order to gain relevant knowledge in consideration of the role itself. In other words, someone can be completely book smart and not have the ability to establish any connections or rapport with his workers, negating any confirmed competency that he may presume that he has in that particular area.

Why? Because no matter how much he can quote from a book or what he can solve, if it cannot be managed and cultivated within a particular field and through the appropriate channels of human capital, it will never be successful ensuring that he will be seen as not having any knowledge in his role as the potential leader within the organization or company.

A candidate can help improve the perception that she knows much about the intended role that she seeks by involving herself in nearly every aspect of the department or company, learning from those in the "trenches" how the intricacies of company systems work? What completing the work entails? What are some of the positives and negatives related to the systems?

Further, when candidates take on multiple tasks at the same time, an evidenced high level of proficiency leads to the perception that the candidate understands all that needs to happen to help make others within the office or company either just as—or even more—successful than she is.

IS THE CANDIDATE A TRUE LEADER?

Does the individual hold himself daily to interacting with other members of the organization within a certain set of values? Is he seen as trustworthy and loyal to a cause, or if he is elevated? Will he now share all of the water-cooler "secrets" with upper management? Is he kind and helpful when members of the team are in need, and does he lend a hand when time constraints create a pressure chamber for the team and there is no help in sight?

Individuals perceive a true leader as someone who exhibits such care and compassion for his team that his team would walk through a wall for him. A true leader is perceived as someone who understands what the team is expected to deliver, and understand what it takes to help move obstacles to ensure that the team gets there.

A true leader is an individual perceived by others to give up his time for them - to make their plans priority over his so that the rest of the team will continue to be motivated to perform in such a way so that success can be realized by all parties, moving the company or organization forward.

CAN THE CANDIDATE MAKE DECISIONS?

Is the individual able to make informed decisions and willing to take the consequence for her actions or does she hem and haw? This is an extremely important consideration that colleagues and other individuals will take into consideration when reviewing how they perceive you will be as a manager or leader. In order to navigate this correctly, the candidate must work to ensure that all decisions are made in a timely manner and with some type of informed process in order to prove that data and feedback is used to make these choices.

Even something as small as choosing where to eat lunch and the process used to lead that decision can be perceived as weak, strong, or forceful in nature. In that scenario, are you taking the likes and dislikes of others into consideration, as well as time, cost, etc. It sounds like an irrelevant example, but this actually sums up this entire chapter perfectly—everyday is an interview. That includes nearly all of the interactions you have with others and how they perceive you to be in the role.

IS THE CANDIDATE A GOOD LISTENER?

Another extremely important trait that exemplifies a potential good leader is if she is a good listener. An individual must be perceived as being successful in navigating workplace issues by listening to her co-workers and constituents in order to obtain knowledge and feedback to make the most informed decisions and ensure that people always feel included.

It is also important that potential subordinates and colleagues know that you can listen to their personal issues and offer advice and support for their troubles. The leader of a company or organization can sometimes be equated to a parental "unit," as the care and oversight of a department, district, team, company, etc. is considered a "family" of sorts, and the leader's power and influence can assist members with giving appropriate direction.

Of course, good listening skills are important in any relationship. But as a leader, listening is important to the strength and dedication of the team. To be perceived as a good listener, the leader will in fact ensure that his colleagues and subordinates understand that their opinions, ideas, and concerns are important to the mission and success of the team as a whole.

Being perceived as a poor listener means that the individual is also a poor communicator and will not have the support needed to be successful in the workplace or industry. Even if he doesn't agree with what the individual is expressing during the dialogue, his ability to listen and, in turn, open the lines of communication are what will be remembered, respected, and discussed among the rest of the team and throughout the workplace.

DOES HE BRING WITH HIM STRONG ALLIANCES?

The strength of a leader is measured in the competency and value of the team he builds in the workplace. If the leader already has strong alliances who have the knowledge base and respectability of a company, department, or an industry as a whole, he brings with him an appropriate and proper respectability and belief in his team right from the start. Being perceived as having strong alliances will also automatically set the political stage for him as well. The connections of the initial alliance will also provide secondary and tertiary relationships that will act like tendrils in consideration of fostering relations and moving the mission forward.

Although this is important connectivity when discussing navigating workplace politics, the relationship and ancillary connections don't always bring with them positive feedback. Usually, colleagues and subordinates are skeptical of alliances especially if they arrive from outside an organization where "proper" vetting is minimized.

The initial perception of outside alliances brought into teams after a transfer of power includes the immediate sour "smell" of political tribute or a spoils system that maintains a level of cronyism one would hope to avoid. However, by including the team in the transition of the new member and the restructuring of workplace systems that will insulate the department, the "fear" will be short-lived as this ally proves her worth through her actions and productivity while mimicking the same values that the leader possesses and caused him to elevate to that role.

IS SHE A RISK-TAKER?

This can be valued either way. In a company, organization, district, etc., risk taking can be beneficial at times to personnel, productivity, and output, while at other times risk can be seen as unnecessary, unsafe, or jarring the status quo. While navigating the workplace, it is best for her to be perceived as a leader or colleague who is confident in her decision-making process since it is backed by the input from her team and industry/subject research while still having the ability to push the envelope for the good of the organization. Individuals who are seen as too conservative can be labeled as "lazy" are uninterested in "moving the needle" toward higher standards.

However, this type of navigation must be performed at a slow and steady pace to ensure sustainability. If it is perceived that she is too much of a risk-taker, team members and subordinates may feel uncomfortable in the possibility of placing too much at stake which can diminish the level of respect that she has worked so hard to create. An individual must weigh out the pros and cons in consideration of the effect the risk will have on the individuals on her team and the team as a whole.

WILL HE SUPPORT HIS SUBORDINATES?

The perception around the proverbial water cooler and in online forums must include how the candidate will definitely support his team and subordinates. "He's one of us," must be the outcry from the cubicles. "He won't forget 'where' he came from." The easiest way to lose support in a leadership role is to stop supporting the individuals you lead. I think that is definitely worth repeating as it is a key mantra to live by when striving for the loyalty and backing of one's colleagues and others around the organization.

Supporting colleagues and subordinates doesn't mean to always agree with them. Rather, it is usually closer to the opposite. Even an incredible idea or plan can only get increasingly more defined when it is being challenged by other individuals who also want to see everyone succeed.

CHECKING FOR UNDERSTANDING

How Are You Perceived?

- Where would you rank as a candidate in consideration of what was discussed in this chapter?
- What can you do in a professional sense to help make "you" more marketable on a daily basis?

Chapter 13

Perception and Planning (Short-Term and Long-Term Goal Setting)

Every great leader uses short- and long-term strategic planning goals to ensure the mission meets the vision of the organization or business. In planning for success, it must be perceived by constituent groups that these goals have a solid foundation and are attainable. Having "a plan" ensures others that the leader is organized and can be perceived as having long- and short-term expectations for himself and the other members of his leadership team and the organization as a whole.

Regardless of a field or career path, every individual should have some idea of where she sees herself in both the near and distant future. By doing this, she forces herself to plan out daily functions and future engagements to provide a strong outline for a successful venture to fulfill that goal. It is important to understand that these goals are not permanent and can be modified as different situations arise throughout one's livelihood. Thus, in dissecting this further, one could understand why short-term goals may change more frequently than an individual's established long-term goal setting.

Long-term goals help strengthen the perception that the leader of a community is placing much emphasis on remaining in the role for a sustained period of time, creating a feeling of stability among his constituents. When an individual exhibits much interest in meeting a goal that will take some time to accomplish, it can affect the amount of "bye-in" others have when moving forward to attain said goal.

This can be an important power play for aspiring and established leaders alike, in that the ability to motivate others to meet the goal over an established timeframe leads to more organized work production and greater potential for output since there is an outline of specific timelines to meet in keeping on target to meeting this long-term objective.

Short-term goals give the perception that the leader is working on specific tasks to make some type of deadline or achieve a particular status in a more immediate fashion. Many of these goals are what is known as "low hanging fruit," and the individual can make a serious impression on others if most, if not all, of these goals are attained and met quickly. Establishing a short-term goal also lends itself to encouraging strong work ethic, communication, and team building between subordinates which will only help in strengthening the work unit as a whole.

However, it will only be perceived as a successful and organized venture if these goals are attained. In knowing this, a successful leader understands that he must create goals and a goal-setting strategy to ensure that his team reaps the benefit of seeing his goals come to fruition. This can be accomplished in several ways.

CHOOSE GOALS THAT HAVE SHORT DEADLINES

When establishing a short-term goal, the time frame must be kept to a minimal span from start to finish. This is important since the leader wants everyone to recognize the goal and bear witness to the successful outcomes and the process it had taken to get to those outcomes. Short-term goals do not fare well where procrastination sets in; rather, this type of goal should have a short turnaround time so that an organization, company, or an individual can utilize the success that can be realized in minimal time to effectuate a near immediate change.

This especially works well when an individual is trying to impress her superiors, a client, or is attempting to calculate next steps. Some examples of goals with short deadlines can be creating sales routes, introducing upcoming programs, enhancing facilities, and working on safety issues.

ENSURE THAT SOME TYPE OF TANGIBLE REWARD CAN BE NOTICED

It is necessary that the outcome of an established short-term goal can be measured in some way that can be noticed from individuals both outside and inside the firm, district, or organization. Whether monetary in nature or just a public commendation, a notable advertisement of the goal's outcome allows others to invest in your successes and revere others who also were successful with you because they help you reach this goal.

By causing others to wait for an outcome due to complexities that are established by the creation of the goal, it is simple to lose all of the original excitement that had been built up in the first place to help others perceive that the leader is effective in the organization because his goal was met and met without pause or any stumbling blocks that couldn't be overcome.

On the other hand, when a short-term goal is established, worked on, and then completed without any publicity, write-up, or accolades from other individuals in the workplace and out of the workplace as well, it is time to re-evaluate how perception plays a key role in determining how others perceive the success of the leader. Others, especially those outside the organization, must be informed when the goal is met and how it has moved the vision and mission forward if the leader wants to be perceived as successful

LEAD THROUGH THE DECISION-MAKING PROCESS

As has been the mantra of this book throughout the previous chapters, it must be perceived and evidenced that a leader continues to lead by example and takes part in placing all of the theories of leadership and management into true practice. By doing so, she must maintain the utilization of best practices to help advance both her own standing in an organization and the organization's mission as a whole.

This is no different when decisions must be made in helping to define short- and long-term planning. The individual must ensure that she directs all components of the plan in order to attain a projected outcome. When establishing a short-term goal, she must consider using a directed informational approach to invite feedback and input from all associated stakeholders while maintaining control over how the goal is reached. Short term isn't synonymous with "fast" either. It is important that each and every goal is well-thought, includes appropriate resources, and has an appropriate outline and action plan to ensure success.

It must also be perceived that feedback loops will be in place and utilized throughout the entire decision-making process, and the data analyzed must be taken into consideration to make necessary changes and complete action plans. Ensuring that immediate members on the team as well as other stakeholder groups take part in the decision-making process brings the planning full circle and will generate greater acceptance of the methods behind what it takes to make appropriate decisions for successful completion of goal.

CHECKING FOR UNDERSTANDING

How Are You Perceived?

- What are some of your short-term professional goals? Long-term?
- How are some ways that professional goal planning coincides with personal goals?
- What are the pros and cons of having too few or too many goals?

Chapter 14

Words of Power and Promise to Be (or Not to Be) Perceived As

In studying the history and definitions of words in the English language that represent power and promise, a leader or aspiring leader, in any business or organization doesn't need to be a wordsmith in order to recognize that there are particular words that can be perceived as a strength or a weakness to an individual's ability to lead or make decisions. True, it ultimately depends on the utilization of the word and its context. However, by pure definition one can wholly understand how the utilization of such independent devices can cause someone else, whether it be a stakeholder or member of a constituent group who is a supporter of or against a cause, to perceive how a leader is reacting to a particular situation.

In fact, power words do not only reflect what is written but also how one is perceived as acting when a particular situation arises. The chart below outlines twenty of the most influential words/terms used to describe leadership actions or how leaders themselves are perceived when carrying out a decision-making process that affects both themselves and others.

It is interesting to note that as many of these terms stand alone, we can define them as being either negative or positive in how each is represented on the surface. Then, as we consider each definition more holistically and insert it in different decision-making situations, one can begin to understand how a specific definition can relate to an industry weakness or strength dependent upon how the leader needs to be perceived.

In looking to navigate the workplace and be successful in attaining established goals, an individual must know these terms and how they can be perceived at any given time. Further, it is important to realize that these actions and roles can (and should) be used differently when moving from one job, goal, activity, and the like, to the next.

Table 14.1   Perception

Perception	Perceived as a Strength	Perceived as a Weakness
Leader	X	
Doubt		X
Advise	X	X
Advocate	X	X
Coach	X	
Consult	X	
Inform	X	
Resolve	X	
Humble	X	X
Hurt		X
Love	X	X
Fear	X	X
Acquire	X	X
Enforce	X	X
Inspect	X	X
Surpass	X	X
Lobby	X	X
Target	X	X
Screen	X	X
Vet	X	
Monitor	X	
Review	X	
Align	X	X
Revise	X	X
Investigate	X	X
Empathetic	X	X
Empower others	X	X
Risk	X	X
Guarantee	X	
Merge	X	X
Be Admired	X	
Exploit	X	X
Compromise	X	X
Wealth	X	X
Conservative	X	X
Calculated	X	X
Balanced	X	X
Arrogance	X	X

CHECKING FOR UNDERSTANDING

How Are You Perceived?

- Choose five of the Power and Promise perceptive terms from the list (table 14.1). Now reflect on your job or industry and a project or work goal that you recently completed. How did each of those five areas play a role in your decision-making efforts and the outcome of the project as a whole?

Chapter 15

Learning from the Leadership of Others

Change Leadership vs. Change Management

A true leader grows stronger with more experience and specifically more knowledge of how other leaders make mistakes. The only true successful leaders are those who can come to the conclusion that what she has done she could have been done better, and by doing so her leadership ability grows stronger.

Each and every one of us will at some point in our lives face certain obstacles. Those who aren't complacent and continue to work toward perfecting what it is they truly need and desire will always be prepared and remain successful during change. Leaders take important steps toward decisions—it is how they deal with the outcomes and responses to those decisions that truly matter.

Many leaders are never truly satisfied with the norm and instead will be looking for change in their professional lives so they will know in advance when a change is approaching. This is a type of change leadership. Others will allow themselves to become comfortable and not remain focused on the change that is going to occur. This is defined as change management. There is a huge line drawn to separate change leadership and change management. In fact, the distinction between the two is actually quite significant, and individuals strive to be perceived as change agents to advance their navigating the workplace hierarchy.

Change management refers to a set of basic tools or structures intended to keep any change effort under control. The goal is often to minimize the distractions and impacts of the change. Change leadership, on the other hand, concerns the driving forces, visions, and processes that fuel large-scale transformation. Here, we see why the leadership piece versus the management tool is so important to keep separated. It is the vision that constantly changes with the needs of the organization and the people in said organization who keep the formula alive where learning about the role of the leader in the organization only helps others become and even feel more successful.

Learning how to learn, innovate, and change are all closely related. The notion of "change" is arguably the most powerful because it focuses on results and implies proactive movement from one place to another. There's leading through normal times, and then there's leading an organization through a change. One might be tempted to say that there's no difference between the two, but that would be naïve. Change leadership has its own demands and requires a different mindset and an extra set of capabilities in order to lead the organization to a new place.[1]

Everyday leadership is not easy, and I don't mean to dismiss it as such. It takes a special type of person to motivate employees throughout the organization, drive toward results, satisfy investors and analysts, and hobnob with partners and influencers. On a different scale, leading a function, unit, or division, such as Sales requires its own set of abilities and discipline, including greater attention to detail and keeping sales managers and reps focused on hitting their number on a weekly, monthly, and quarterly basis.

Leadership and being a true visionary can only come about by ensuring the perceptions of our roles are not only spot on, but become a successful link between the expectations of both the leader and his followers. There is a perceived, innate desire and need to fulfill the mission and at some point change becomes the reality.

This condition is the way we learn—the way it is. However, one must consider that all the necessary components of being a leader and a change agent for the good are intended to make both the leader and his constituents successful. Successful leaders are only successful when they cannot ignore the fact that it is those days where success only comes from change that impacts the way the leader reacts to any and everything that affects his unit.

Change is scary—change is difficult—but change is good. Change is also extremely necessary. A leader that doesn't change is a leader who will not be effective. As leaders, we must remain active and participate in the tenets of the definition or fall stagnant and let change interfere with how we move around the maze of life.

Leaders must be perceived by all as everyday agents of change. In most cases, a leader will have a faction of colleagues and subordinates who do not support him in the role, and he will have a number of others who will be in complete awe of his prowess and emulate every move. One's ability to serve others while allowing them to take responsibility and credit for all of her accomplishments is the most effective way for any leader to be perceived more as a proponent of change leadership as opposed to change management.

As one navigates her workplace politics, maneuvering through the use of devices that support the role of how perception leads to an individual's success, being known as an agent for change, can sometimes help and other times hinder following through on the established goals and principles of her position or office. Some workplaces, structures, departments, and programs need an individual to come into an operation and grow it, at times in a drastic fashion. Other times, the status quo should be maintained until appropriate observations and input can be realized, and decisions for change can be made.

An individual must navigate steadily while being careful not to endure the wrath of gossip-seekers or pessimistic workers who may label her with the microaggression of being too strong-willed, overly aggressive, or even too headstrong. This must not occur for several reasons, most important because she will be perceived as too "bossy" or ineffective, and may cause alarm for other managers higher in the company structure so as to be concerned that she is looking to take their jobs.

Rather, she must use her change leadership style and measure it at a consistent place, constantly observing the markers of how she is being perceived by others. This can only be achieved with assistance from alliances and her own ability to adjust the manner in which she interacts with others to ensure she is invoking the right message. An individual shouldn't change her style and beliefs system in order to be perceived in the preferred manner as prescribed in the tenets of leadership. In turn, being perceived correctly and using her own skills to "spot" how others are perceived will help her manage the political environment.

CHECKING FOR UNDERSTANDING

How Are You Perceived?

- What are three things that a leader can do for his constituents to be considered an effective change agent?
- Why is change so difficult to accept?
- Describe a time when you were affected by a change in a policy or procedure at work? How did you react to the change? What would have made you react differently?

NOTE

1. Kotter, J. P. *Power and Influence: Beyond Formal Authority.* New York: Free Press, 1985.

Chapter 16

Culture, Perception, and the Workplace

Culture is central to understanding an individual's beliefs and expectations. This also holds true for the culture that revolves around the work environment. It is solely evident that shared culture, values, and goals influence the diversity of ideas and may create a mixed response to change. It is further evident that culture-signifying attachment to a specific place or job may suggest that there is something beyond personal relationships with others that bonds individuals to the places in which they live and work.

Specific mention of social capital and interactional methods allow individuals to maintain the idea that different perspectives invite different theories to support the definitions behind cultural beliefs and understanding. First, we can compare how different views of human interaction converge or diverge in relation to each other in understanding one's potential to participate in a local community. In applying the concept of community field to local communities, examples align with the thought that community field is community development:

It is development of the community rather than development in the community.[1] Specific circumstances within a community can cause the structure of that community to change. From an interactional perspective, a community is composed of several distinct social fields that pursue specific interests. The "community field" is distinct from other social fields because it does not pursue just one single interest; rather, it pursues a general interest(s) of the entire community. Therefore, it is the actions of a community field that coordinate and organize the actions of other social fields into a whole.

Wilkinson (1999) defines community field as a process of interrelated actions through which residents express their common interest in the local society (p. 2). The emergence of the community field is affected by the context of local life, but more directly is facilitated by the interactions among the diverse residents of the locality.[2] The community field cuts across organized groups and across other interaction fields in a local population. It abstracts and combines the relevant aspects of the special interest fields, and integrates the other fields into a generalized whole.[3]

The interactional approach does not define community in terms of networks or systems. Rather, the local groups are conceptualized as "unbounded fields of interaction."[4] The community is composed of several of these distinct social fields.

As an example, Bridger and Alter (2006) find that in most communities, it is possible to identify social fields focused on different aspects of local life such as social services, economic development, recreation, and public safety. The mechanism that links the various special interest fields to local society is the community field. Therefore, as these different social fields begin to converge within a community, strong bonds are developed helping to clearly define the culture of the community.

Another example of creating culture with the investment of individuals via bonds and other relationships is "place theory." Galiano and Loeffler (1999) define "place" as simply "a geographic area that has meaning to people." In fact, the social science research surrounding "place" has been a complex, widely diverse model used by many to describe the bonds within a community.

Place Dependence is used to evaluate one place as compared to other places, to determine the level of agreement with the idea that, particularly due to emotional bonds, "no other place will do as well as this one," or a dependence on the particular place of interest for the things one wants to do.[5] The community relationships described are important to both the individual bonds of the community and the success of the community as a whole.

The focus of a second "place" concept, the *Place Identity* concept, is that "this place" is part of my identity; my affiliation with "this place" is part of how I want others to think of me.[6] Here, we see evidence of how a person "becomes" part of his or her community. There is a strong affiliation between both what the community and individual represents. We see this with religions and cultures that follow religious beliefs and traditions as a daily means of living.

As we relate to these perspectives and understand the theories behind culture and the expectations of individuals within diverse communities, one also can envision how these perspectives contribute to understanding how well-being emerges within communities themselves. This is the basic function of social capital. While social capital is generally an agreed upon topic, two identified perspectives can surface regarding a "profit" from the capital received—whether this profit is accrued for the group or for the individuals alone.[7]

Social capital has resonated with a wide range of audiences, largely because it holds the promise of effectively replacing the "primordial bonds" that held communities together in simpler times.[8] Specific community bonds and capital can be affected by people within the community based on the needs of the individuals or the culture they share with other factions of the community.

Take, for example, strong social capital in certain ethnic groups that can dominate industries, while excluding other ethnicities from certain trades and even keep cultures down through what is termed as "downward-leveling" pressures. "Rumors and boycotting of a business are often based on tensions between community groups, rather than on the service or goods it provides."[9]

The implicit consensus is that social capital is important because it allows people to work together by resolving the dilemmas of collective action.[10] It is extremely important to the well-being of a community dynamic and perspective that social capital commands resources in order for it to have a true meaning within the community structure. Social capital that is fractured creates a major distraction in the community and damages well-being. Thus, the way to rebuild social capital is by fostering participation among all members of the community,[11] in turn, strengthening cultural capital defined as an asset embodying cultural value.[12]

Tangible cultural capital consists of material things such as buildings, structures, sites, and artwork while intangible cultural capital comprises a set of ideals, practices, beliefs, traditions, and values which serve to "bind" people together.[13] In finding these ties, Levitte (2004) and Woolcock and Narayan (2000)[14] point out the importance of "bonding" social capital as a support system where "bonding," or familial or "strong ties" refer to people one knows well and are often the first source of help when a business owner, board chairperson, or community individual fails.

The researchers further described "bridging" as expanding into additional community networks and networks of acquaintances. Bonding is necessary to expand community businesses and free members from obligations that may hurt economic potential.[15]

Bridging, on the other hand, is important for keeping business and the community stable and sustainable where people share knowledge about the business community by word of mouth and distinct conversations. Levitte continues to note that the "lack of bridging and linking networks can be restrictive to economic development efforts" (p. 47) which would also limit the growth of the entire community.[16]

Hence, we come back to that immediate question where there is something beyond personal relationships with others that bond individuals to the places where they live. The ties of the community are strengthened once again through the integration of beliefs, traditions, and values behind those mechanisms.

CHECKING FOR UNDERSTANDING

How Are You Perceived?

• What three words describe the culture of your workplace??
• How do you value social capital?

NOTES

1. Korsching, P., & Allen, J. (2004). Local entrepreneurship: A development model based on community interaction field theory. *Journal of the Community Development Society* 35(1): 25–43.

2. Brennan, M. A., & Israel, G. A. (2008). The power of community. *Community Development* 39(1): 82–98.

3. Wilkinson, K. P. (1999). *The Community in Rural America*. Middleton, WI: Social Ecology Press.

4. Bridger, J., & Alter, T. (2006). Place, community development, and social capital. *Journal of the Community Development Society* 37(1): 5–18.

5. Ibid.

6. Ibid.

7. Lin, N. (2001). Building a network theory of social capital. pp. 3–29 in Lin, N., Cook, K., & Burt, R. S. (eds.). *Social Capital: Theory and Research*. Hawthorne, NY: Aldine De Gruyter.

8. Coleman, J. (1993). The rational reconstruction of society. *American Sociological Review* 58(1): 1–15.

9. Levitte, Y. (2004). Bonding social capital in entrepreneurial developing communities – Survival networks or barriers? *Journal of the Community Development Society* 35(1): 44–64.

10. Portes, A., & Landolt, P. (1996). The downside of social capital. *The American Prospect* 26: 18–21.

11. Schafft, K., & Brown, D. (2003). Social capital, social networks, and social power. *Social Epistemology* 17(4): 329–42.

12. Throsby, D. (1999). Cultural capital. *Journal of Cultural Economics* 23: 3–12.

13. Ibid.

14. Woolcock, M., & Narayan, T. (1998). Social capital: Implications for development theory, research and policy. *The World Bank Research Observer* 15(2): 225–49.

15. Trentelman, C. (2009). Place attachment and community attachment: A primer grounded in the lived experience of a community sociologist. *Society and Natural Resources* 22(3): 191–210.

16. Ibid. at 9.

Chapter 17

Competency

Being competent is the ability to do something skillfully and efficiently. Successful leadership is a phrase that must be synonymous with competence. In order to navigate a workplace and be perceived as an effective leader, an individual must exude a high level of competency in several different areas in order to achieve a respected status in consideration of an organization's hierarchy and the value that he brings to the said organization.

Although exhibiting a high level of skill in particular areas can provide insulation for a leader when his decisions, plans, and management style come into question, it is nearly impossible to maintain the notion that a sense of confidence in a certain level of skill exists without the leader being able to perform that skill set almost perfectly each and every time he is called to do so. With this, he will be perceived as having an intrinsic level of knowledge to lead in the specified area and his overall competence will grow within the organization.

So, let's be very clear—an individual or especially, an aspiring leader or manager, cannot "fake" his way through a test of competency when a skill or methodology comes into question. In fact, it is extremely relevant and important when dealing with competency checks for the leader to examine his weaknesses and fully understand what areas he should look to improve. Knowing this isn't an overall weakness; rather, it is an important method in assuring one is being perceived with a certain level of expertise that will help him lead more effectively.

In knowing which skill or action would stand out more than likely when an individual, or a group of individuals from internal or external means, questions reasoning behind some process, the leader can look to avoid discussing or spotlighting that area when questioned or provoked. We all need to work on something, and understanding where one's strengths and weaknesses lie is detrimental to strengthening the perception that others have of that individual's competence to serve and to lead others.

For example, one area where competency levels in leaders can change drastically and almost overnight is with advances in technology. A leader can be known as competent in the area of a program or piece of hardware as she utilizes the equipment and software as a current productivity piece to analyze, measure, and formulate data trends on products and program initiatives. Further, this can be shared among peers and used to compare metrics with similar companies and organizations who may be viewed as competitors.

As with any "new toy" the program carries all the "bells and whistles," and it surpasses industry standards as the leading software to exponentially grow profit margins into the new year. The leader receives advanced training and professional development, but she knows that she does not have a high level of competency to provide the necessary, successful delivery of every function of the program.

Here, she must use her skills set in order to be perceived by the group that she is capable and competent of implementing the program that she has chosen to be responsible for. This can be accomplished by extending the "spotlight" to others and allowing her subordinates to play an integral part in professionally developing an aptitude in the subject, device, program, etc. for the rest of the group.

In doing this, she not only ensures that optimal training is reached, but she is also perceived as facilitating greater morale among her team by inviting others to take charge of particular components of leadership. Her being perceived as delegating duties to others for their benefit (to be permitted to play a leadership role in and take charge of a program initiative) shifts any perception away from her that she is unable to extend the necessary training and information effectively to her team on her own.

What this shift ultimately does is change the narrative from being unable to fully provide the level of competency needed to reach a desired goal to delegating authority to strengthen the team through turnkey trainings provided by competent workers in the "trenches." Not only has the leader effectively met her mission, but she has also enhanced respect from her team.

During this process, however, the leader must remain actively involved in every component of the training she has just established. In other words, she just can't choose a place and time and then leave. It is crucial that she introduces the training session; explains the reasoning behind choosing that exact program, application, and the like; provides some background on the features and benefits from the program; and ultimately provides a strong introduction for the trainer, firmly establishing his expertise and competency in what he is training.

Further, it is vitally important that throughout the session, the leader interjects at appropriate intervals to either reiterate something the trainer says/does or relate the purpose of the topic to some practical component of the task at hand. It is equally important that she refrains from interjecting too frequently so as to disrupt the flow of the transference of competency from the trainer to other subordinate teammates. Should this occur, it would most likely be perceived as an insecurity on the part of the leader in allowing another individual to add to the value of the vision of both the leader and her organization.

Whatever the case may be, establishing a high level of perception in the area of competence is extremely significant as one navigates the landscape of his workplace. This holds true in every facet of the job from speaking and writing, to engaging others, through all related interactions. Holding oneself to a high regard is essential in assuring that there is a critical understanding as to how competent an individual is in her performance along with a cogent argument as to why she should hold the position she does.

A high degree of competency also surpasses any other component necessary for success. One can argue that several qualities must all collide within an individual in order to ensure that success can be measured; however, without competency there would be no "glue" to hold the framework together. As we have focused in the periphery of these chapters on leadership and the perceptions of leaders in the workplace, let us excise competency from one of the needed qualities for assuming that role.

Can you then identify many incompetent leaders? To be fair, you can pinpoint where certain incompetency and impatience played a role in their demise. However, a leader who enjoys success at some point or another in her role had first had to prove that she reached (or be perceived as having reached) a high level of competency to effectuate change within her organization or department.

A certain respectability comes along with her proof of competency, and this will allow her to continue to move through the workplace or organization when formulating further initiatives or trying to advance an agenda for herself, her unit, or the company as a whole. As one tends to understand that a certain level of competency must be attained in nearly every successful task in life, it is most important that she is perceived as being competent in the eyes of her colleagues and subordinates in the workplace.

This can really only be achieved if there is a high level of awareness and a dedication to the goal of enhancing her competency through specific measures that will expand her aptitude on a specific subject or topic. This can be accomplished through self-guided research, additional training, and most important, keeping current with industry/career trends in order to maintain a relevance that will cause her to be perceived as connected with the team.

Other important things to consider would be to pair up with peers within the industry; join organizations and associations relative to the field; continue to seek certifications and degrees through avenues of higher learning; mentor colleagues and subordinates; subscribe to current and relevant peer-reviewed periodicals and journals; publish articles, papers, and manuscripts; and strengthen technological literacy through the expansion of a knowledge base in advanced programs and pertinent applications. In all, the more one can do to cast a wide net around events and activities that will enhance competency in a particular area will only help her navigate the workplace more effectively.

CHECKING FOR UNDERSTANDING

How Are You Perceived?

• What are three important areas of competency for a leader or manager?
• Reflect on a manager or supervisor you have worked with. What made you perceive him/her as competent? What actions describe an incompetent leader or supervisor you have worked with?

Chapter 18

The Gold Standard Rule

Question before Comment

The "golden rule" for any successful individual to follow is to question before comment. This most definitely should be the mantra for not just all leaders, but members in nearly every corner of society. The rule also provides a foundation that should be established for every relationship—both personal and private. In too many instances, individuals tend to speak without thinking, and act without knowing. The idea of asking enough questions before making your decision about something or commenting about an individual action is only proper in consideration of one's ability to "win" in a situation or in the very least, not look unintelligent or uninformed.

USE RESEARCH AND DATA EFFECTIVELY

There are too many avenues and technological applications to justify not using data and research to question an individual or entity in consideration of any topic that may concern interested parties. Society's fast and accurate ability to "fact check" and disseminate response via social media has made challenging an individual, especially in the public domain, a more difficult task than decades prior. In the past, the perception was made that any individual, who seemed to have a handle on a situation or just "looked" the part, was telling the truth every time she made a comment or answered a question.

Thus, when she was asked a question, her answer was always "right" regardless of the answer that was given. Even if her answer was disputed at a later time, there was no efficient way to spread information to others that she was wrong in a timely manner. Therefore, the back-and-forth question-and-answer sequence truly had no consequence for either side except that every audience had to believe what it heard at face value.

Today, there is an automatic shift in that thinking since we have become a world where "Googling" someone or something has become second nature. Fact-checking has taken on somewhat of an art form, and careers and industries have grown from our need to prove ourselves right or others wrong in a most immediate fashion.

This can be seen in the political arena, nearly every workplace, and in almost every social circle where the simple use of a smart device at your fingertips can provide immediate discovery and instant feedback to a question or dilemma that is raised. Thus, acquiring data streams and pertinent information prior to questioning an individual on a work-related issue that may have a detrimental outcome to an individual and his standing in consideration of workplace politics will not only be beneficial but is an absolute necessity.

Here, one can truly understand the importance of ensuring the right information is obtained and used prior to making a comment. An individual must be perceived as having the correct knowledge base to challenge an individual on a topic. Too many times, the question asked can be viewed as political in nature, unseeingly removed from the topic at hand, and detrimental to one's standing on the organization. To be sure, one must understand wholly that at times, it is better to refrain from getting involved in challenging someone with a question than asking any question at all.

KNOW THE ANSWER BEFORE
YOU ASK THE QUESTION

As stated earlier, research and data must be obtained, reviewed, and analyzed to ensure an informed decision can be made on what type of question should be asked and if the question should even be asked at all. Along with this, it is imperative that said research leads the individual (asking the question) to the correct answer as well. Although it seems matter-of-fact, a leader or any individual cannot underestimate the importance of ensuring that she knows the correct and full answer to the question she is asking. This is important for three reasons.

First and foremost, she must ensure that the appropriate question is asked so that she is perceived as having control of the situation at hand. On many occasions, when individuals concentrate on the question they are asking they find a need to attenuate the question or change "directions" either to ensure it aligns with fact-checking standards or is covering all bases.

Second, a question must be reviewed for proper utilization before it is delivered to confirm that the question will not provide any "wiggle-room" for the individual charged with answering said question. If the idea is to ask a question in order to invoke a specific answer or comment, the more direct it is the less space available for the individual to maneuver his way out of answering the question. This holds true in both cases where the individual you are questioning is either friend or foe. Providing an ally with a very direct, "softball-esque" question can help him be perceived as knowing the answer and avoid any stutter sequence or confusion.

For a person who is not an ally, assuring that a question is direct enough to strangle any attempt at her maneuvering around the intended answer is an important tactic in aligning oneself with the appropriate question to quell how she may be positively perceived by others. This is extremely valuable as one decides that one wants to land the question with the intent to damage an adversary.

The third thing to consider when deciding the right question to ask prior to commenting on a situation at hand is if the question, in the decided form, can cause the individual to be positively perceived and gain power. In other words, will the question that is asked causes the individual to look more intelligent and better prepared because of his ability to answer the question that was asked? This may be what the intent was all along; however, if the prompt was posed to deter or negatively affect the individual, then the wrong question can absolutely backfire on the person asking the question.

In all, it is most important to question before commenting on a topic to ensure that the intended outcome is reached. In an audience, one who attempts to confront or question individuals can be perceived as having an agenda— whether it is to help or hinder an intended cause. Regardless, choosing the right format, diction, and tone are all important matters to decide when one is using perception to navigate the politics that surround the workplace.

SO, WHY NOT COMMENT FIRST?

When one comments without questioning first, it can tend to look like a political agenda is being put forth on the individual being questioned. It can also be easily perceived as one individual trying to "catch" another in either a lie or not knowing the answer to the question. If this is what he wants perceived, then an initial comment is a good way he can get his point made and "steer" the direction of the dialogue as a "first-strike" method.

However, more than often, and especially if he is commenting on something that is coming from a seasoned individual, the comment can be refuted or rebutted in such a way to ensure that it looks political or he looks uninformed. This can be (and it will be) detrimental to the way he is perceived by different members of the company or organization, and the fallout may be difficult to overcome the next time he chooses to approach an individual on a topic with an actual question.

Hence, commenting can be seen as an interrogation if he does not have all of the information readily available or is unsure that a good response can be given. With a question or questions leading up to the comment, one is perceived as trying to gain the necessary knowledge to assist an informed decision.

After the questions come forth and are answered, a follow-up can even extend how he is looked at by his team. This is also a prime opportunity to ensure that the polioptics don't favor a "set-up" of sorts since it will look as though the natural order of questions then comment has put him in the best position to assist the other individual instead of attempting to block him or catch him off guard.

Other times, when one decides to comment first before having the information she needs, the straightforward attitude can be perceived as aggressive, disloyal, and not wanting to be a team player. She may indeed be some or all of these things; however, she must want to learn the power of perception to maintain the element of surprise as she navigates her workplace.

Too many individuals comment on ideas and actions without anticipating the answer they will receive. With minor preparation, one can be successful in meeting her goal of catching another individual off guard while strengthening the perception of her gaining information to advance the vision of the organization.

Remember—always take a breath! There is not much in life that needs to be answered or acted upon in some immediate fashion. It is always beneficial to take one step back, survey the situation at hand, and then take one more step backward. Choosing to gain as much knowledge on a topic while being able to direct the conversation in the direction it needs to go is the optimal stance in any situation that craves conflicting dialogue. Why not comment first? Simply because it is not always necessary. It is better to develop a situation into one's own terms rather than backpedaling and apologizing later.

CHECKING FOR UNDERSTANDING

How Are You Perceived?

- As a self-reflection, do you tend to comment on something first so as to give your stance or opinion before you ask a question?
- Can you recall a time when commenting first hurt your status in an argument or discussion? At what point did you recognize that this tactic wasn't working? What could you have done differently?

Chapter 19

Using Perception to Navigate Workplace Politics

The foregoing chapters have provided an outline for several important areas for one to consider as he realizes the importance of how he is perceived throughout his workplace. In studying these tenets and applying some of the major concepts to specific fields and industries, an individual can attenuate the text to assist in advancing his own agenda forward, helping him maintain stability and a firm awareness of what is necessary to be successful.

The concept of politics in the workplace is real, and the individuals who learn to sift through the political fodder and determine what is needed to strive inside will always be successful. The perception of their prowess and their ability to circumvent any hurdles that are established to thwart progress will release any doubt that they are a formidable force to be taken seriously throughout the organization.

As is certain in any classroom, building, factory, camp, office, or annex around the globe, our perception of others tends to guide how they are treated, what responsibilities they are granted, which positions they can hold, and in what promotional titles they are competent to excel. These perceptions are what will be used to evaluate the performance of said individuals, and the outcomes will be scrutinized and analyzed to dictate their future in the outfit while outlining some proposed trajectory of their path around the workplace.

Where politics and perception intersect is where an individual must interpret what is most important to him in consideration of his standing with work colleagues and subordinates. In lies the rub, as one must be sure to choose wisely when attempting to curry favor or entice another individual for something that is beneficial and supportive of his own needs. Being able to decipher what is needed and read the cues and clues that are set forth will give him an upper hand when using perceptive mechanisms to make decisions necessary to meet and surpass the standards set by the organization.

CHOOSING ALLIANCES

Choosing appropriate alliances with colleagues will help ensure that an individual will have a support system in place while attempting to maneuver through any political tensions or obstructions. However, when choosing allies one must be sure to choose wisely. In the workplace, alliances do not always need to be matched based on personal preference or likeability. Rather, alliances should be matched based on the sole purpose of their ability to quickly, efficiently, and accurately complete the prescribed goal or mission.

In other words, members of a true alliance do not seemingly need to be friends with one another. Instead, there must be a mutual respect between all alliance members and an ability to at minimum act cordially toward one another throughout the relationship.

Although being a friend, as opposed to being friendly, with members of an alliance may seem the preferred method, at times alliances will "shift" based on the changes to the political landscape. When this occurs, a close relationship with a friend, who may now be seen as an adversary, can cause issues in consideration of information that was previously shared, contracts that are binding, and other pertinent actions and agreements that will now be suspect due to the change in the relationship.

What helps more is to steady an alliance based upon a symbiotic relationship where members interpret the needs of others by knowing what each needs for himself. Loosely stated, it is no secret that at some point each individual in a workplace or organization will need some assistance with a matter that skims a political lens and most likely, will seek that assistance from an individual with whom he has aligned.

In turn, one must establish what the relationship will give in return, and what it will take to continue the relationship. What's more, the individual should decide what is most important from the alliance and set the tone by creating the relationship rather than waiting for someone to approach him first.

BE AWARE OF MICROAGGRESSORS

There may be no other word that perception is more closely tied to than microaggressor. Although this term usually depicts forms of microaggression based upon factors of indirect, subtle, or unintentional discrimination against members of a marginalized group, they most certainly are conditional to how the group is perceived by oneself based on outside influencers rather than actual data points.

Examples of microaggressors that are most commonly known to society include things like "your name is so hard to pronounce," or thinking that anyone who is of Latinx descent can translate a phone call or document. Other aggressors identify groups of individuals who are ethnically "smarter" than others, and calling a female boss "hysterical" which is a major sex-linked bias.

In the workplace, microaggressors such as these and others are important to avoid for numerous reasons relative to human resource issues alone; however, as one continues to use perception to navigate her workplace, it is also important to view microaggressors in a different light as well so as to ensure that she forms the clearest picture of each work associate in her mind.

Where most microaggressors and tones associated with these aggressions tend to be discriminatory in nature, a master in perception can also use these same aggressors to gain his own needed momentum and invoke a certain response from others. These can be based on race, gender, age, orientation, or disability.

In the same manner, an individual should not make an automatic or natural decision on someone or some action based on what she perceives to be true based solely on a microaggressors. I recall a situation in my youth as a new college professor teaching writing to a class of adult learners at night, some more than twice my age. Most of these individual students had immigrated from other countries and as English was not their native language, writing becomes an even more difficult task to conquer where English grammar is nearly impossible to master.

After the fifteen weeks was over and the last class had ended, a female student, who had struggled early in the class but vastly improved at the end of the semester, handed me a thank you card and a brief discussion ensued. Probably, fifteen years my elder, she went on to explain that she was a quantum physicist in her country, earning her doctor of philosophy degree years prior to teaching at a prestigious university.

The conversation was an epiphanic moment for me in my early life since I realized that, prior to that moment, I had used microaggressors to dictate my rationale for others. Not once did it cross my mind over the course of fifteen weeks that this individual could have been anything more than a laborer just trying to make ends meet and finding time on her own to afford several classes to help her with her English.

In fact, this student of mine was much more advanced in her education and career than I was. I perceived her to only be different because of her lack of aptitude in the English language.

To provide a clearer path to the message in this section—never underestimate an opponent. Not suggesting that individuals should be opposing colleagues or others in the workplace, but competition is fierce, widespread, and cutthroat in certain businesses and industries. Whether it is for the most important accounts, the best "leads," the corner office, or—yes—that promotion you are hoping for, an individual can never let her guard down where politics are concerned.

Be aware of the microaggressors that are perceived for others and if they are true to form as expected. In many cases, some research and observation will assist in determining what is reasonable and what is completely off base. It is important to recognize that these aggressors can both benefit and hurt individuals seeking leverage for tasks, activities, and the like.

As they are revealed and utilized to one's advantage, others must be careful not to incite any negative publicity or backlash moving against what has been established. Rather, just recognizing where each individual in an organization stands will help identify any potential concerns in the near and distant future.

KNOWING WHOSE BAG TO CARRY

One may have heard the anecdote, "Yea, he got that job because he used to carry her bag." The scene is clear with the image of a woman in a suit being followed three steps behind by an awkward man carrying her oversized brief-case or satchel while they are whisking to work. Realistically, the picture is a perfect metaphor for knowing who to back and how to back him where one can gain the most benefit.

It's true that some workers overdue it. Laughing at bad jokes, bringing the boss coffee (every day), and other actions that define the quintessential "brown noser," always looking to please the "higher ups."

But in recognizing an understanding of the underlying meaning, one can always have knowledge of who around the office is important to pay attention to. When deciding alliances and other political devices, knowing who to extend your loyalty to can mean all the difference. Most times, once a decision on who to support is made, those backing the individual will always be perceived as supporting her. Therefore, if and when the culture shifts or another individual acquires a transfer of power, it becomes near impossible to carry someone else's "bag." Thus, should one choose to make this type of commitment, he should choose wisely.

KNOWING WHEN SOMEONE IS
ALSO PLAYING POLITICS

As one begins to utilize his own and some of the aforementioned tactics and per-ceptive measures to navigate his workplace, it is beneficial for him to be able to ascertain when someone is using some of those same tools and devices against him as well. Just as he has become a master student in navigating workplace politics, others are using multiple perceptive measures to do the same thing.

In facing any formidable opponent, the only way one comes out on top is to know what his next move will be. Further, he must never underestimate the will of someone who wants the same things from the organization as he does. When an individual makes a conscious decision to do whatever she needs to get what she wants, it is time to ensure that her drive is not taken for granted or ignored in any way.

Even "little things" always lead to "bigger things" if left alone when they should be addressed. Therefore, being able to identify the nuances or triggers in any individual looking to motivate and influence the political environment of the workplace will give an observer the ability to map out where the proverbial trail leads to and dismantle it as necessary.

It is beneficial for an individual to be cautious when identifying someone trying to work a political angle. Moving in too fast with a maneuver to halt and address a political motive means that an individual would "show his cards early" and lose the element of surprise while tracking the entire progress of the full plan. Further, an individual who makes his move quickly must be sure that he is correct in what he is challenging and is using the same methodology to diffuse the issue through a wit and admiration that will still maintain a stealth modality should the return of the attack be unfavorable.

Conversely, moving too slowly or out of an overabundance of caution can actually help an adversary or rival maintain a strong support base or, even worse, grow his support base since others in the workplace could pledge their loyalty should they perceive that no other individual in the company or organization is challenging him.

Also, when one identifies a political maneuver or type of coup and waits to act on it, she may cause a snowball effect of other tactics to follow, gaining momentum and becoming difficult to halt if it goes on for too long. Although moving slower in challenging rivals or adverse methods should always be preferred over moving too fast, an appropriate balance must be maintained as navigating the workplace becomes synonymous with monitoring the way others navigate it as well.

KNOWING WHEN TO SAY, "WHEN"

Giving in isn't always a weakness—waiting around too long is. It is understandable that in any venue where a competitive spirit exists, any type of resistance or challenge can last until every resource is exhausted. This is not an uncommon instinct that we have as human beings, and the drive intensifies as we enter more competitive arenas like the workplace.

Although a strong will and fierce outlook is what is needed to succeed against an opponent, there will come a time when it is more relevant and opportunistic to step back and review what the current outlook is in order to make an informed and very crucial decision of whether to stop persisting and monitor a new plan of action or just steady the course.

As we have discussed patience and one's ability to research and analyze data points to make informed decisions, the exact same thing holds true when deciding to step back from a situation at work. Whether it is an initiative not working as planned, an intense disagreement or conflict with a peer or subordinate, or an overall idea you weren't too fond of that looks as if it has more support than expected, the absolute best tactic to maintain control and a firm handle on the situation is to stop pursuing the outcome you were striving for and to settle on the alternative.

Kicking and screaming because something didn't go the way it was planned can be an exhausting prelude to failure. If an individual can ensure she is perceived as not being affected by the "loss," then she can change the narrative to effectively support any change that will be coming her way. Hence, if done correctly she may never have to reveal that she had originally backed the other idea, plan, or interest.

Again, attenuating one's plan of attack or being subtler with some of the reasons she is moving in another direction may not always be the wise choice; however, she must choose her battles based on the outcome she will receive and how it will affect her future dealings in the workplace. Worrying about how this individual decision will impact future decisions is what's really important here.

HOW OTHERS SHOULD BE PERCEIVED
IN THE WORKPLACE

This book has been created to help students of workplace politics use perception to navigate some of the interactions and daily dealings with personnel and other areas of productivity. Within that environment, it is necessary to remember that others are using their perceptive measures to make a permanent mark on their successful navigation as well. To understand those roles better, one should also look to examine the benefits and ulterior motives that others are seeking through their need to be perceived in a certain way.

CHECKING FOR UNDERSTANDING

How Are You Perceived?

• What types of microaggressors can you identify in your workplace?
• Think about some of your professional alliances. What are the strengths and weaknesses of each member?

Chapter 20

Perception Is Key

A medical emergency during an afternoon run finds a father being rushed to the hospital via ambulance one ordinary Saturday in June. In pain, he clutches the stretcher answering questions for the emergency technician who is preparing him to be received by the ER. Although the trip seemed to take forever because the pain was unbearable, in less than ten minutes he reaches his destination and is escorted out of the vehicle and into emergency Bay 23.

Nurses begin to monitor vital signs and an intravenous line is inserted as the emergency medicine doctor approaches in her mask and scrubs asking, "So what happened? Tell me about today?"

Immediately, the doctor is perceived to have the training and requisite knowledge to perform the necessary tasks to make the father feel better and relieved of his pain. And initially, it is purely because the doctor is in the appropriate clothing, asks the right questions, and must be "good" or the hospital wouldn't let her see him. Along with her confidence, she exudes a competency level and commands the respect of her surrounding team which helps to solidify that he must be "in great hands."

This father also trusts that others have made the hard decisions about her and her aptitude in the profession since they awarded her a medical degree and hired her at such a prominent hospital. Because of how she is perceived, he has no clue until after his discharge that that was her first week at the hospital. But would that have mattered?

For the doctor, she used her expertise and her ability to communicate to navigate the workplace to make it into that ER. Although she earned it, she continues to need to be perceived by others that she is competent and qualified every time she enters Bay 23 as well as every other patient she sees while at work.

She strives to ensure others in her field to respect her, and she craves an instantaneous moment of being revered for what she has accomplished. She understands that how she holds herself and how others perceive her will dictate her ability to serve them effectively as well as earn the esteem necessary to surpass the daily requirements in her career while wading through the politics at work.

This is just one example of the numerous interactions we encounter on a daily basis where perception becomes reality and affects the progress and outcome of the successful future that an individual has within her organization or company. Along with how important the role perception plays in our own lives, decisions that include the role of others create a similarly important need for those other individuals to be perceived in such a way to ensure their credibility and status in their position or field as well.

This arguably holds true in every workplace or industry in consideration of a global marketplace where workers, managers, CEO's, laborers, staff, and others posture to provide evidence and stature to ensure that they are perceived as having the foundation, tools, and stamina to handle the duties prescribed by their office or job in the most effective manner. Just as favorable is the need and desire for them to be perceived within the internal affairs of their actual organization in such a way so as to clear all obstacles and delays when navigating around political capital and the decisions and actions associated with their workplace.

The preceding chapters contain theories, best practices, and tried-and-true methods for individuals to recognize and make use of while attempting to find their way through the politics of their workplace and to compete with others who use politics as a catalyst to motivate, restrict, or coerce co-workers and higher level leaders into perceiving themselves in a certain way.

As was first set forth in the opening of this book ("Why Read This Book"), perception is key for any individual who is wanting to utilize his strengths and core values to help promote a change within an organization; formulate a strong and positive stance for how he is viewed by others at his job or within his company; motivate others into thinking he may be more prepared or competent in an area where he may not be as strong; enhance how others view him in consideration of future leadership or management roles; and grow strong alliances due to how he is respected and revered by colleagues, co-workers, and subordinates.

The preceding pages further analyze the reasoning behind our utilization of perceptive measures and how perception relates to many of the tenets of leadership, comradery, and the management of organizational systems throughout business and industry. Through an examination of the key role perception plays in the workplace, the text outlines some critical areas for the everyday worker, seasoned manager, and an aspiring or already established leader to help her identify specific and important strategies and devices to help her be successful, including the following:

- Perception is defined differently across careers and industries as well as the changing role perception plays in specific organizations and careers. From private business and the not-for-profit sector to government positions and educational venues, the art of perception can be viewed in different ways and must be used effectively within specific circumstances. A truly effective leader is one who is able to recognize a need and use perception to his/ her advantage in any organization of business culture.
- Polioptics or the visual art of perception which identifies and defines the visual tools of perception that can be utilized to navigate workplace politics and assist leaders as they move to elevate through different leadership "chairs" within their fields and/or organizations.
- What are workplace politics and how to navigate it successfully by putting theories into practice while ensuring that an effective leader is using perception to assist with the engaging of tasks, moving the mission forward, and motivating staff members. It is easy to read the concepts and gain knowledge of the subject to assist in the transition of any leader and leadership team; however, putting those theories into common practice to successfully motivate constituent and stakeholder groups can sometimes become an arduous task.
- Becoming aware as a leader and preparing to address political motives and other perceived actions that can cause a mission to fracture and cause problems for the individual leader.
- Modeling every skill set she possesses so that constituent groups continue to perceive her as relevant to the other members of the organization and those individuals who surround the team with the hope of elevating to a leadership role. Modeling not only shows subordinates how the mission should be accomplished but that she is truly proficient in consideration of the matter at hand.
- Taking pride in each and every aspect of his performance, the leader will be perceived as an extremely successful individual. Even those individual leaders who are struggling within different areas of their organization who hold their composure are only perceived to still be extremely effective, in control, and part of a successful business/organization of which others would wish to contribute to or become more involved.
- Using perception to navigate the political aspect of leadership in the workplace gives a competitive edge in considering the ability to persuade others by using perceptive measures to accomplish tasks and motivate subordinates. Each and every decision must result in a positive outcome in order to be perceived as successful.

- An individual's diction, grammar, and syntax are true perceptive measures that influence others when making decisions. A higher order diction forces a client, subordinate, colleague, constituent, etc. to perceive that she has the intellect and knowledge to operate a successful organization or perform the prescribed tasks of her job.
- Every day is an Interview! An individual who is looking to navigate the political atmosphere of any business or industry and elevate to certain positions within the leadership hierarchy must understand that every work day, every decision, and every alliance is being measured in consideration of the vision of the organization or business. The perception of how that leader prepares to be part of that elevated role is critical to a successful outcome in consideration of any promotional opportunities in the workplace.
- Short- and long-term strategic planning goals ensure the mission meet the perceived vision of the organization or business.

Most often, perception is the true office reality, and how one is perceived by others can dictate where her standing in any position will be. Leaders must recognize how they are perceived and work to positively strengthen those perceptions in order to continue to elevate in the workplace and navigate the political environment. Knowing the art of perception is the key that unlocks the future successes for any leader. Like any art form, it continues to reach perfection the more it is practiced.

CHECKING FOR UNDERSTANDING

How Are You Perceived?

- Name three things you learned about using perception to navigate workplace politics.
- Name the most important area you personally need to work to improve in consideration of how you are perceived by others.
- Why is how you are perceived important to you both personally and professionally?
- Describe how you believe you are perceived by others.

About the Author

Dr. Richard D. Tomko has had numerous administrative responsibilities during his twenty-year career in educational administration. He has been a building administrator at the middle and secondary levels and responsible for district-wide curriculum, assessment, innovative program initiatives, technology, and professional development while in central office positions. Dr. Tomko has dedicated his career to serving communities as an educational leader, acting as a director, assistant principal, principal, assistant superintendent, and superintendent in both private and public school systems. He earned a Doctor of Philosophy degree in educational leadership, management, and policy from Seton Hall University; earned a Master of Jurisprudence from Loyola University Chicago School of Law; and holds certificates in community and economic development from the Pennsylvania State University and The Brain, Mind, and Teaching from The Johns Hopkins University. He is an adjunct professor at Manhattan College teaching in both the School Building Leadership and Counseling programs and works as a consultant to educational institutions and families.

Dr. Tomko and his wife, Jaimie, cofounded WISPER (We Invest in Strong Programs, Empowerment, and building Respect for Women), a 501(c)3 established to assist and recognize individuals and their mentors who deserve support in helping to fulfill the mission of "Paying it Forward" by leveling the proverbial playing field in the spirit of equality for all through the advancement of leadership; nurturing of future career paths; representing community ideals; and enhancing academic standards in education.

Dr. Tomko is a change agent for creativity and problem solving and works with administrative teams to decrease achievement gaps between demographic subgroups of learners by involving families, stakeholders, and community groups in the restoration of student engagement leading to overall student success.

www.ingramcontent.com/pod-product-compliance
Lightning Source LLC
Chambersburg PA
CBHW061829220326
41599CB00027B/5235